Using the Newspaper to Teach ESL Learners

▼▼▼▼▼▼▼▼▼▼▼▼▼▼▼▼▼▼▼▼▼▼▼▼▼▼▼▼▼▼▼▼
▼▼▼▼▼▼▼▼▼▼▼▼▼▼▼▼▼▼▼▼▼▼▼▼▼▼▼▼▼▼▼▼

Rafael A. Olivares
Queens College
City University of New York

 International Reading Association
Newark, Delaware 19714, USA

Director of Publications Joan M. Irwin
Managing Editor Romayne McElhaney
Associate Editor Anne Fullerton
Assistant Editor Amy Trefsger
Editorial Assistant Janet Parrack
Production Department Manager Iona Sauscermen
Graphic Design Coordinator Boni Nash
Design Consultant Larry Husfelt
Desktop Publishing Supervisor Wendy Mazur
Desktop Publishing Anette Schuetz-Ruff
　　　　　　　　　　　　Cheryl Strum
　　　　　　　　　　　　Richard James
Proofing Florence Pratt

The diagram "Context and Cognitive Load" on page 12 is reprinted by permission from J. Cummins, "The Role of Primary Language Development in Promoting Educational Success for Language Minority Students" in *Schooling and Language Minority Students: A Theoretical Framework,* published by the Evaluation, Dissemination, and Assessment Center of the California State University, Los Angeles, 1981.

Library of Congress Cataloging in Publication Data
Olivares, Rafael A.
　Using the newspaper to teach ESL learners / Rafael A. Olivares.
　　p.　cm. — (Reading aids series)
　Includes bibliographical references.
　1. English language—Study and teaching—Foreign speakers. 2. Newspapers in education. I. Title. II. Series.
PE1128.A204　1993　93-988
428'.007—dc20　CIP
ISBN 0-87207-237-1: $9.00

CONTENTS

FOREWORD

The role of the press as an educative institution has long been recognized. As early as 1831, the French historian de Tocqueville, during his visit to the United States, noted the role of newspapers in the new democracy he had come to observe. In his masterwork, *Democracy in America,* de Tocqueville wrote, "Newspapers therefore become more necessary in proportion as men become more equal and individualism more to be feared. To suppose that [newspapers] only serve to protect freedom would be to diminish their importance; they maintain civilization." Thus, the press was recognized by this noted scholar as an essential force binding together for a common cause individuals who were otherwise isolated.

Media organizations have taken to heart their charge to be guardians of democracy. This commitment is evident in the long tradition of working with educators and literacy specialists. The concept of cooperative press and school programs is actually quite old. The earliest known reference to the idea occurs in an article which appeared in the *Portland (Maine) Eastern Herald* on June 8, 1795. Educators working with students of all ages have probably welcomed original documents such as newspapers into the instructional program since the publication of the first daily newspaper in London, England, in 1702.

In 1932 the first ongoing Newspaper in Education (NIE) program was established by *The New York Times* in response to the requests of New York City educators who asked if newspapers could be delivered to schools on the day of publication. During the ensuing decades, the NIE concept spread extensively so that today more than 700 ongoing programs are conducted through cooperative efforts of newspapers, schools, universities, and literacy centers throughout North America and selected areas of other continents.

Since the early 1980s, members of the International Reading Association and its regional, state, and local councils have assumed the leading role in encouraging the use of newspapers in teaching, with the peak of activity taking place during the first week of March, when NIE Week is observed. During NIE Week students of all ages and their teachers celebrate the value of reading and learning with newspapers.

In *Using the Newspaper to Teach ESL Learners,* Dr. Rafael Olivares makes an important contribution to the literature on the use of newspapers in teaching. Based on a solid theoretical framework from the fields of linguistics and language acquisition, the instructional approaches suggested include newspaper activities appropriate for second-language learners of several levels. In addition, the text presents an overview of the theory for using the newspaper to integrate language instruction into the content areas. It should be noted that this collection of activities is the result of the author's experience in teaching limited English proficient students and in bilingual teacher education as well as the result of an extensive review of the existing NIE literature for second-language learning. Finally, the appendix includes a helpful list of other resources on the use of newspapers in ESL and content area classes. Using the theory proposed in this book and the information provided in the appendix, readers can explore further uses for the newspaper in the education of nonnative English speakers.

Betty L. Sullivan
Newspaper Association of America Foundation

INTRODUCTION

The growing diversity of school populations in many areas of the world is placing an increasing demand on educational services. In the United States, many schools—especially those in urban districts—serve students who come from a wide variety of cultural, ethnic, and linguistic backgrounds. To address the diverse needs of these students, teachers are beginning to look for alternative instructional materials to supplement the traditional textbook.

Since newspapers are a type of print material that students—nonnative speakers of English as well as others—will use throughout their lives, they are an ideal instructional resource. With many newspaper companies developing educational activities, with hundreds of publications espousing the use of newspapers in the school, and with Newspaper in Education (NIE) programs existing in many countries to promote the idea, newspapers have become well-established fixtures in many classrooms. However, despite the availability of numerous teachers' guides for using newspapers with mainstream students and the wealth of books and journal articles that discuss the academic rationale for using newspapers in the classroom, there has been little if any discussion of the theoretical basis for using newspapers in the education of limited English proficient (LEP) students.

Bilingual and English as a second language (ESL) teachers in the United States have been using the newspaper in their classrooms for some time. Both English-language and minority-language newspapers in the United States have suggested activities for using the newspaper to teach LEP students, either in English or in their native tongue. But until now no publication has presented a comprehensive rationale to support the use of newspapers as an instructional tool for these students.

Newspapers can be a magnificent resource in the education of LEP students. For one thing, the newspaper's physical characteristics are tailor-made for classroom use. Newspapers can be marked, cut, pasted, colored, and discarded easily; since new issues appear daily, there is a constant supply of copies that can be submitted to the same treatment. Another benefit is that English-language newspapers can be used to teach LEP students not only basic language skills but also knowledge of content areas such as math, science, and social studies. And because of the immediacy of the newspaper's content, students develop language and academic skills within a real and relevant context. Newspapers also provide important information about how the community operates, reporting on politics, legal and social issues, employment, health care, and other aspects of society that are generally not discussed in textbooks. Finally, newspapers provide LEP students with a day-to-day representation of the less formal aspects of the mainstream culture. Because they see arts, food, sports, and entertainment in the newspaper, students new to the culture get a feeling for what people do with their free time.

In order to provide practical suggestions based on solid theory, this book emphasizes using newspapers in the context of broader classroom methodologies that have proved successful in the education of language minority students. In developing these practical activities, the book stresses three main elements of research in this area: (1) how second-language acquisition and second-language learning occur, (2) the connection between learning in the content areas and the acquisition of the second language, and (3) the value of the cooperative learning approach in developing language skills.

Because the classroom activities provided are firmly grounded in theory and research in second-language acquisition, this book is an excellent source of instructional ideas not only for bilingual and ESL teachers but also for any mainstream teachers who have LEP students in their classes. (Although the focus here is on using English-language newspapers in English-speaking societies, these ideas may be adapted for use with language minority students in any society. In addition, many of these activities lend themselves to use with newspapers written in the students' native language.)

The book is organized into five chapters. Chapter 1 presents teachers with some background on current theory in second-language acquisition and learning and draws connections between research and practice. Classroom strategies appropriate to the theory are discussed in chapter 2. Chapter 3 suggests specific activities that teachers can use to facilitate the development of language arts skills in the second language. Chapter 4 discusses how and why newspapers can be used to help LEP students acquire knowledge in the content areas. This chapter also describes strategies that can be used to link language acquisition and content area learning. Finally, chapter 5 provides classroom activities that make use of the newspaper to teach mathematics, science, and social studies concepts as well as language skills.

CHAPTER
ONE

The General Theory

Any book that makes recommendations for classroom practice must be based on sound pedagogical theory to be effective. The activities presented in this book are specifically designed to comply with the most recent findings in language acquisition and learning, second-language development, and related fields such as psycho- and sociolinguistics. This chapter reviews those findings to help teachers understand the theoretical underpinnings of the strategies and activities discussed later; with this knowledge, they will be better able to apply, adapt, and extend these activities to meet the needs of their students.

Language Acquisition and Learning

When discussing how a second (or third or subsequent) language is learned, it is important to distinguish between language acquisition and language learning. Research in linguistics shows that there is an important difference between these two functions in both the first language (L1) and the second language (L2).

Researchers define language acquisition as the process by which our minds appropriate the sounds, symbols, and representations that constitute a language. With L1, this acquisition occurs unconsciously as language is picked up from the social environment. When children first begin to use language, they do not pay attention to the rules and structure of the tongue. Their acquisition of the language is focused solely on communicating—on giving meaning to a message. When children are able to recognize some rules and regularities in the language and apply those regularities to new utterances, then we can identify the process of language learning.

The distinction between language acquisition and language learning in L1 is important because the same distinction can apply to L2. But although acquiring and learning a second language entails the same linguistic steps as acquiring and learning the first language, there are some major psycholinguistic and sociolinguistic differences between these processes. For instance, the age of the learner is an important factor when it comes to L2. A very young child will acquire the second language differently than an older child will. Linguistics research has proved that even though younger children seem to acquire L2 sooner than older children and are often able to speak the new language without an accent after a few months, older children and adults are actually "more efficient language learners" (Hakuta & Snow, 1986). The common myth that very young children are better than older children at picking up a second language is the result of focusing observation on pronunciation and phonics, which are mainly functions of language acquisition. When the comparison is made with other aspects of language proficiency—such as the type of language ability needed to succeed in school—older children come out ahead. According to Collier (1987), children between the ages of 8 and 12 learn a second language faster than children between the ages of 4 and 7. This may be because older children have more cognitive maturity and more skill with the first language to draw on in developing an effective second-language learning process.

One of the most important lessons from linguistics research to keep in mind is that in the long run LEP students with a well-developed first language will perform better linguistically in L2 than those students who discontinue their development of L1 and discard its use. Because the language-learning skills developed in L1 can be transferred to the learning process in L2 (Thonis, 1981) and because research demonstrates that bilingual children have more and higher level cognitive skills than monolingual children (Baker, 1988), in recent years educators have supported the idea of having LEP learners maintain their first language as a means of improving learning in the second language.

Another factor that makes the acquisition and learning of L1 different from that of L2 is the influence of the learner's personality. Everyone who has tried to speak another language knows how embarrassing it can be to make mistakes when you're trying to communicate. Outgoing people with strong self-esteem are much more likely to overcome such errors and to involve themselves in interactions that will expose them to the second language (Brown, 1987). Because they are afraid of making mistakes and looking silly, people with a strong sense of social sanction or who are worried about losing face will make less of an effort to use L2.

During the acquisition of the first language, this factor is not as important. Very young children are generally unaware of their mistakes in language use because adults are willing to accept those mistakes as long as they understand the intended meaning. Whether children are shy or outgoing, most adults around them will strive to facilitate communication, accepting any form in which a message is presented. Gestures, other body language, and sounds will be interpreted as part of the child's language acquisition process. With the exception of very young children, this type of uncritical acceptance is not common for LEP students in the school environment. Adults in the school will usually stop the flow of communication to correct errors, emphasizing the message's form over its content.

Other differences in acquiring L1 and L2 can be found in sociolinguistics. Languages carry some social status within societies (Ruiz, 1991); this status can affect people's attitudes toward their own and other languages. If the second language has a higher social status for students than their native language, they may end up adopting L2 as their sole means of communication and rejecting their own cultural heritage. Lack of development, loss of proficiency, and eventually total abandonment of the first language can isolate language minority students from their families and their communities, thus creating sociological problems associated with group adaptation and psychological problems involving personal identity (Beardsmore, 1982).

Teachers must keep in mind that these psycholinguistic and sociolinguistic factors can create affective "filters" in the language development process in school. These filters can become barriers that must be lowered in order for language acquisition and learning to occur (Lessow-Hurley, 1990). For example, a shy student may avoid participating in the classroom, which can hamper learning. In some ethnic groups, children are taught to listen to adults but not talk to them. Consequently, in those cultures to be a good student is to be silent and listen to the teacher. In these situations, the affective filter interferes with the classroom dynamics necessary for second-language acquisition. Specific recommendations for overcoming these affective filters are suggested in the practical sections of this book.

Understanding Meaning

The differences between language acquisition and learning and between developing L1 and L2 are at the core of the theoretical framework behind the teaching methodologies used with LEP students. For Krashen (1981), one of the most prominent researchers in this field, the distinction between second-language acquisition and second-language learning is central to understanding how LEP students develop language skills in L2. He hypothesizes that real fluency in a second language is the result not of learning L2 but of acquiring it. Thus, he stresses the need for communication and interaction in the classroom. He suggests that acquisition occurs when we understand the language; and understanding comes from paying attention to the content of a message, not to the form. Because stressing grammar and syntactical structure emphasizes form over meaning, that approach is not as effective.

Krashen (1982) also suggests that learners acquire a second language by working out messages that are a little beyond their current language capabilities—a technique that allows them to add new information to their repertoire one piece at a time. This "input hypothesis," as Krashen calls it, contradicts the principles of the audiolingual approach. The audiolingual approach, one of the most popular methods of teaching ESL over the past 30 years, relies on drills of scripted interactions. This approach is based on the idea that students need to learn the basic structures of L2, which is why it stresses drills and practice of language patterns. Because it emphasizes structure, the audiolingual approach makes it difficult for learners to focus on the content of the message. Of course, the use of hypothetical interactions designed to help students internalize language structures does not provide the same linguistic experience as natural communication. Most of the time the fast-paced interaction in a real conversation does not allow time for participants to pay attention to form.

Researchers in second-language instruction note that when a teaching methodology stresses form at the expense of function, it does not leave room for the learner to develop a "comprehensible input" of language. In other words, if instruction focuses on specific language patterns rather than on content, learners will have little attention left over for discovering new words, new structures, and new patterns in the second language. Under these circumstances, the principles of learning outlined in Krashen's input hypothesis are not at work.

Although Krashen's main points have held up over time, recently he has been criticized for overemphasizing the role of input in second-language acquisition. Most current researchers accept that learners must comprehend input to acquire a second language, but few agree that comprehensible input is all that's necessary (Larsen-Freeman, 1991). Swain (1985), one of Krashen's early critics, suggests that second-language learners need not only to comprehend the input but also to practice producing comprehensible output in the second language.

Regardless of the continuing debate over these points at the theoretical level, teachers should keep in mind that all this research points to the fact that LEP students need to develop second-language skills through participative classroom activities. No one disputes that these students, like any students, need to communicate in a meaningful way. The interpretation, expression, and negotiation of meaning required for participative classroom activities will force LEP students to develop communicative competence (Savignon, 1991).

Second-language acquisition from a communication perspective demands the use of language in context. This approach for L2 acquisition is consistent with the whole language approach to reading instruction. Again and again, research has demonstrated that in order to learn any new form of communication it is more important to understand the message (content) first and to focus on the structure of the code (form) later. At the classroom level, ESL methodologies that emphasize language structure over content are more concerned with how to teach those structures than with how students acquire them. In other words, the focus is on the teaching process rather than on the learning process. And that is a mistake.

On the other hand, content cannot be expressed without form. In order to decode a message and give a meaning to it, one must know and understand the code. To some extent, this understanding marks the transition from language acquisition to language learning. In real interaction situations at the classroom level, LEP students will not have the chance to monitor their use of language or to focus on the code. For that reason, they will be acquiring language more frequently than learning it. Since the goal of instruction for these students is to help them acquire *and* learn language, some focus on the structure of language is necessary—as long as it remains secondary to the content.

Building Students' Proficiency

Cummins (1981) has developed several additional concepts that should be built into any theoretical framework for the instruction of LEP students. Cummins's work complements Krashen's but approaches matters from a different perspective. Using as a reference the research on second-language acquisition and learning, he distinguishes two types of second-language proficiency: basic interpersonal communication skills (BICS) and cognitive academic language proficiency (CALP). Without these two proficiencies, he argues, LEP students will not succeed in the school environment.

BICS are kinds of skills LEP students acquire from their interactions with peers, from the media, and from day-to-day experiences. BICS allow the L2 learner to communicate in colloquial conversations; they are the language survival skills. However, BICS are not enough to succeed in a classroom environment, where the communication process frequently requires cognitive skills in the second language and usually demands the use and comprehension of context-specific concepts. For these uses, second-language learners need a more complex and comprehensive set of language skills; this is where CALP comes in. If a second-language learner can process communication with very little context, he or she has reached the CALP level. Once they have achieved this proficiency, learners can understand and apply abstract concepts in L2 as well as make use of thinking skills and strategies in that language.

To explain the relationship between the nature of a communication and the context of the communication process, Cummins (1981) suggests a continuum in which communication goes from context embedded to context reduced. Context-embedded communication is full of environmental or context clues. An example is the interaction between a foreign tourist and a salesperson in a fruit market. If the tourist wishes to buy something, she does not need too much proficiency in the oral language to give meaning to her message. Gestures, facial expressions, and other body language can take the place of oral language to communicate meaning. More than that, since there is an obvious purpose for the communication and the roles of the participants are clearly defined, the interaction's significance is clear.

At the other end of the continuum, context-reduced communication provides no context clues. The success of the communication—for instance, this book—relies exclusively on the participants' (or readers') ability to decode the message. This can be quite difficult, particularly if the communication introduces an abstract concept, such as language acquisition, that must be defined with other abstract concepts.

To the context-embedded/context-reduced continuum Cummins (1981) adds the dimension of cognitively demanding versus cognitively undemanding situations. This dimension measures how much cognitive skill in the second language is necessary to process the message. When these two dimensions are factored together, we get a diagram on which different types of communication can be plotted (see diagram on following page).

If we observe classroom activities, most of what is happening in the school will fall into quadrant D. Frequently, classroom instruction and textbook work rely heavily on verbal explanations or written instructions that provide few nonverbal clues from which LEP students can infer meaning. Furthermore, since the school system expects intellectual performance from students, most classroom activities are cognitively demanding. Most of the

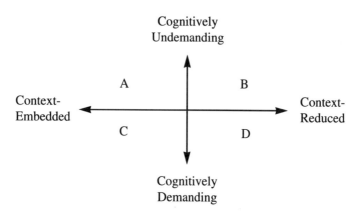

time, LEP students functioning at the BICS (basic interpersonal) level can efficiently process second-language communication only if it falls within quadrant A—that is, if the communication is context-embedded and presented in a cognitively undemanding situation. To function well at quadrant D, as for most school activities, requires a highly developed CALP—in other words, a far more sophisticated level of proficiency. Since by definition LEP students are not fully proficient in L2, they do not have a highly developed CALP in that language and consequently will not function at the expected linguistic level in a regular classroom.

Ideally, ESL methodology should focus on creating a classroom environment in which the interactions and instruction move within quadrant C. Since there are no educational reasons to expect that LEP students will perform worse academically than native English speakers, it is important to provide cognitively demanding activities. At the same time, teachers should be sure to offer an environment full of context clues. This combination can help LEP students learn the second language while developing high-level thinking skills (Romero, 1991).

Applying Theory in the Classroom

All of the classroom activities suggested in this book are solidly grounded in the theoretical framework discussed in this section. Because they are intended to facilitate language acquisition, they require constant interaction among and between the students and the teacher. In keeping with current theory, these activities focus on the content or meaning of language. However, they also provide some guidance in understanding the language structure. During this process of negotiating meaning and understanding the form of the language, second-language learning will occur.

In keeping with Cummins's (1981) findings, the strategies and activities proposed in this book are intended to create a classroom environment that (1) provides numerous context clues and (2) encourages the development of cognitive skills. To achieve both goals simultaneously, these activities allow LEP students to draw on all their personal resources, including their native language and cultural background, to develop their learning and thinking skills.

C H A P T E R
T W O

Strategies for Using the Newspaper with LEP Students

Strategies for organizing ESL and bilingual instruction should draw from both classroom practice and recommendations specific to second-language learning. One of the most successful strategies for organizing instruction for LEP students is the cooperative learning approach, which was developed for use in regular classrooms. Since many newspaper activities are well suited to this approach, cooperative learning is discussed in some detail here.

This chapter also outlines two classroom strategies specific to second-language instruction: the total physical response strategy and the natural approach. Both of these teaching methods have proved effective with LEP students, and both work well with using the newspaper in class.

The Cooperative Learning Approach

Research findings in the field of second-language instruction have shown that one of the most successful curriculum approaches in this area is cooperative learning (Cohen, 1986). Teachers working with LEP students have found the cooperative learning approach effective not only for second-language acquisition and learning but also for instruction in the content areas (McGroarty, 1989).

Part of the reason for the success of this approach in educating LEP students can be found in the distinction between levels of language proficiency discussed in chapter 1. As Cummins (1981) noted, students develop basic interpersonal communication skills, or BICS, in informal situations that provide lots of context clues. Talking with peers, playing in the yard, or discussing personal matters are the kinds of interactions that characterize BICS. These kinds of interactions are embedded in context, making the meaning of the messages easy to understand.

The more sophisticated cognitive academic language proficiency, or CALP, is needed for formal interactions in context-reduced situations. With the exception of the voice of the teacher or the symbols printed in a text, academic interactions tend not to provide many clues to the meaning of the communication. If an LEP student has not reached the language proficiency necessary to understand the text or the formal language of the teacher, that student will be disconnected from what is going on in the classroom.

To help LEP students develop the more sophisticated language proficiency needed to understand abstract academic concepts, teachers must provide a classroom environment that is rich in context clues. In other words, they should create a learning atmosphere in which BICS and CALP can be combined.

The cooperative learning approach can provide such an environment. Working in small groups, LEP students can function comfortably at their BICS level to maintain the flow of communication with their peers. If the group task demands CALP, students who have not reached the required level of proficiency can discuss the meaning with others, and members of the group can help one another understand the learning process involved in the task.

Using the newspaper in such groups can greatly enhance the benefits of the cooperative learning approach. Since the newspaper contains not only alphabetical symbols but also photographs, drawings, and concrete representations of objects, it provides valuable context clues to help students work out the meaning of the group task. This combination of peer interaction and context clues embedded in the newspaper will allow LEP students to perform more demanding activities (and thus develop more cognitive skill) than would otherwise be possible.

Task Structure

At the core of the cooperative learning approach is the principle of effective task structure. According to this principle, the task to be performed should be clearly defined (Slavin, 1983) and structured in a way that allows the group to work out the best way to perform it. This means that the teacher's instructions to the groups should provide as little information as possible about what procedures to use in completing the task. For example, with a problem-solving task, the problem must be clearly stated, but the group should be left to decide on a strategy for solving it.

If a group task is structured properly, it will demand a great deal of interaction among the members of each group. To select the best strategy for completing the task, they will have to discuss, argue, and persuade—all of which require negotiating the meaning of messages. After the students have settled on a strategy, they must continue communicating and interacting in order to perform the task. In this way, a well-structured cooperative learning activity will require the continual production and development of language.

Group Structure

Many teachers have found that when they assign a group task, the work gets done by one or two students in each group, with a large number of students not participating at all. To avoid this situation, developers of the cooperative learning approach have formulated the principle of effective group structure (Slavin, 1983). This principle states that in order to make all group members work cooperatively, it is necessary to assign a role to each member of the group. Ideally, each student will have responsibility for performing a specific task (Kagan, 1987). To do so, they must cooperate with the rest of the students in the group. The result of this process is that the whole group learns.

With this structure, a carefully planned activity can help LEP students with both language acquisition and language learning. By communicating with their peers during the task, students will reinforce the language they have already acquired while picking up new information. Because they will be focusing mainly on the content of the messages, they will be able to acquire language quickly. At the same time, reporting on group activities to the rest of the class will give students an opportunity to concentrate on the form of the language, correcting their linguistic mistakes and thus expanding their knowledge of the language's rules and structure.

This approach also helps lower the affective barriers to developing a second language. When they work in a nonthreatening situation, shy students feel freer to communicate. The active role assigned to each student further encourages interaction. And since the interaction is among peers rather than between the students and the teacher, any cultural restrictions on talking to adults don't apply.

Language Heterogeneity

The theoretical framework for second-language acquisition and learning has met all the practical academic needs of LEP students that have been mentioned so far. However, there are some complications that must be considered. As noted earlier, Krashen (1981) found that second-language learning occurs when new messages are one step beyond the language rules and generalizations the learner already knows. In most classes, this factor is very difficult to control since second-language proficiency can vary widely among students in the same classroom.

Of course, this situation is not peculiar to classrooms with LEP students. Even in a class in which students all share the same native language, a teacher will often note deep differences in reading, writing, and oral language skills. Once differences in students' personalities and learning styles are factored in, the gap becomes even greater.

With LEP students, these differences are compounded because these learners have different proficiency levels in both L1 and L2. Students in separate ESL or bilingual classrooms theoretically should not have huge differences in language proficiency since they are usually tested and placed according to their skills. In practice, however, most LEP students attend classes that are linguistically very heterogeneous.

Cooperative learning can turn this potential problem into an asset. Research in cooperative learning has demonstrated that in order for the approach to be most effective, the groups *must* be heterogeneous (Kagan, 1986). LEP students with different levels of proficiency working together in small groups can practice, develop, and improve their language skills at their own pace. The more advanced students will reinforce and expand their own skills by explaining messages and describing language forms to the less proficient students. At the same time, performing the group task and learning in an environment rich in interactions and context clues will allow the less advanced students to improve their language proficiency.

Total Physical Response

Developed by Asher (1982), the total physical response approach is based on the premise that L2 can be learned through the same process by which L1 is learned. With this approach, LEP students—like young children learning their first language—must respond to commands that require physical movements. At the beginning they are not asked to produce any kind of oral language; instead, they perform movements to demonstrate listening and understanding. After a period of weeks or months during which they acquire and then internalize language structures and vocabulary, students will be able to start producing L2. The assumption here is that with the necessary practice and exposure to language structures, students eventually will be ready to break the L2 code, just as they did with L1. The assumption seems to hold up in practice; total physical response has been used successfully with young children to teach not only English as a second language but also other languages.

A number of activities with the newspaper can make use of this approach. Activities dealing with sequencing (or other aspects of action), the identification of emotions, and practicing sports are particularly suited to physical movement. Working with cartoons or photographs from the newspaper, children can imitate the movements shown and follow commands to acquire vocabulary. Many of the activities suggested in later chapters of this book can be adapted for use with the total physical response approach.

The Natural Approach

The natural approach to second-language instruction was inspired by research into the concepts of language acquisition and language learning. This approach meets Krashen's basic conditions for the acquisition of L2 by providing a comprehensible input and focusing on the communication of messages (Lessow-Hurley, 1990). It also improves students' chances of learning by lowering affective barriers.

In the natural approach speech fluency in the second language is developed in four stages. In the *preproduction* stage, students communicate with body movements or gestures. At this stage students understand but do not produce language. At the *early production* stage, students start using very short phrases and sentences accompanied by body movement to help clarify meaning.

In the third or *speech emergence* stage, students begin to use longer phrases and sentences. During this phase, students will continue using the strategies developed in the earlier stages to get across ideas they can't yet articulate. At the fourth stage, *intermediate fluency*, students are able to interact in conversations and produce connected narratives.

If they adhere to the natural approach, at first teachers will supply most of the inputs without asking the students to produce language. After the students have acquired enough vocabulary to pass the early production stage, and after they have shown signs of mastering some basic structures of language and speech, teachers can start providing activities that require more oral interactions. It is recommended that reading and writing be introduced after students have reached the fourth stage.

Several newspaper activities suggested in this book can be organized by the teacher to follow the sequence outlined in the natural approach. Other activities can be adapted to fit into this sequence. However, because the natural approach is mainly oral and the purpose of this book is to integrate reading and writing as soon as possible, only some of the activities will strictly adhere to this approach.

Classroom Activities to Develop and Reinforce Language Skills

One of the purposes best served by the use of newspapers in education is to provide students with new, informative material while reinforcing language skills already acquired. The activities presented here for developing oral, reading, and writing proficiency in the second language do exactly that: they give students the opportunity to expand their acquisition of English vocabulary and at the same time reinforce language learning. In addition, some of the activities will help students develop specific thinking skills, such as categorizing, classifiy, inferring, and decision making.

Because these activities have been developed on the basis of the possibilities offered by the newspaper, they are not tied to any specific curricular sequence. However, since LEP students vary widely in age and level of English proficiency, the activities are divided into two levels: beginning and intermediate/advanced. Some of the more advanced activities expand on or add another dimension (often writing) to the beginning-level tasks. It is up to teachers to select the activities they think are appropriate for their classrooms and to modify or adapt them as needed to meet the second-language academic needs of their students.

Beginning Activities

1. To acquire, reinforce, and develop new vocabulary in English, students can cut out pictures of familiar foods from the newspaper and then name and discuss the items. To practice classification skills, they can paste the pictures on paper, grouping them under different categories. For a more advanced classification lesson, they can cut out similar pictures from another newspaper and, working in groups, arrange those pictures into new categories. For instance, carrots may come under vegetables, natural foods, or snacks.

2. Working in small groups, students can cut several food items from the newspaper and organize a dinner or lunch by pasting the items onto a paper plate. Ask the students to work together to write the name of each item next to the picture. Students can use these vocabulary terms to say something about what they eat for lunch or dinner. (See Figure 1 for an example.)

3. Using the names of foods cut from the newspaper, students can act out a trip to the supermarket. Taking on the roles of clerks, cashiers, or customers, they can sell and buy the items they've cut out. Since the focus of this activity is on communication skills, teachers should emphasize fluency and meaning in the interaction over how students use the structure of the language.

4. Ask students to search the newspaper for photos and drawings of people performing different jobs. Working in groups, they can identify and label the occupations depicted. At the very beginning levels, students can name the

Figure 1
Activity 2: Organizing a Meal

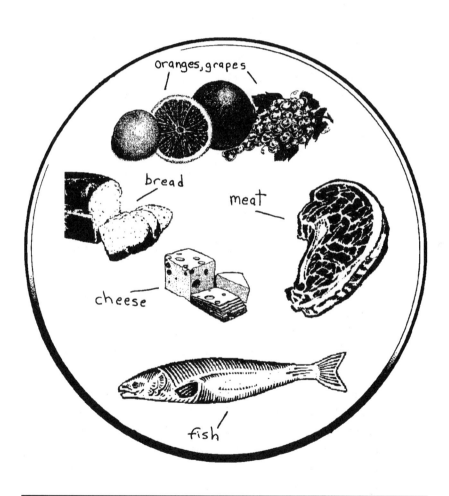

occupations in their native language and have the teacher or a peer in the group provide the English names. (Figure 2 provides an example.) For an extension activity, ask the members of each group to talk about the jobs of people they know. In addition to reinforcing vocabulary relating to occupations, this activity can introduce or reinforce terms such as father, mother, sister, aunt, uncle, friend, and neighbor.

5. Show your class pictures cut from the newspaper of public or private buildings. Ask students to work in groups to name the kinds of jobs people do in those buildings. Encourage them to use any form of communication to identify occupations; English terms can be provided by peers or by the teacher on request. Then have students cut out or draw pictures of people who perform the jobs named and create a class poster connecting the characters to the buildings. Repeat the name of each occupation and write it next to the appropriate picture. The poster can be kept on display for students to refer to later.

6. Ask the students to search the newspaper for pictures of people at work. In small groups, they can discuss and list the kinds of skills necessary for each job and the kinds of activities the job entails.

7. Working in pairs, students can choose a job description from the classified ad section. Have each pair dramatize a job interview based on the information provided in the ad. Let each student play the employee and the employer in turn.

8. Ask the students to work in groups to locate common items in the newspaper as you call them out. Examples might include a car, a book, or an orange. To stress listening comprehension and vocabulary, repeat the words if necessary. When they have found all the items, ask the students to cut them out, paste them on construction paper, and label them.

Figure 2
Activity 4: Occupations

bricklayer

businesswoman

mechanic

judge

welder

Every week, a different group's paper can be displayed in the room to reinforce vocabulary. Be sure to credit the creators of each week's display.

9. Ask each student to go through the newspaper and cut out objects of his or her choice, such as cars, jewelry, or stereos. Then have students role play, giving away or lending the selected objects to other students. Provide them with the necessary vocabulary to practice interactions using complete phrases or sentences. To keep the flow of communication going, do not stress the use of the exact form, even if a student makes a mistake. Allow students to use their native language as a supplement if necessary. Remember, this activity is meant to help students acquire vocabulary in context and gain confidence in second-language interactions. ESL teachers have long conducted this type of activity using classroom objects; the advantage of using the newspaper is the variety and novelty of the objects available. Students love to give and receive items such as cars, boats, houses, and fancy clothes.

10. Ask students to find photographs of people in the newspaper and cut them out. Have them guess what emotions each person was feeling when the picture was taken. Let beginners use body language and gestures to identify emotions. Ask the students to label the emotions and say something about how the person in each picture was feeling.

11. Ask students to look for photos and drawings of different types of clothing in the newspaper. Have them cut out pieces of clothing to create an outfit appropriate for school, for a picnic, and for other situations. They should identify each piece by name, when necessary using their native language and getting help with the English term from classmates or the teacher. Introduce new vocabulary to create phrases and sentences and to keep each word in context.

12. By cutting furniture, appliances, TV sets, and other objects from the newspaper, students can design the interior of a house. Have them work in small groups to draw plans for a house on construction paper and connect the objects they've cut out to the appropriate rooms. (Figure 3 gives an example.) Members of each group can describe their design to the rest of the class. Introduce necessary vocabulary to help students name objects and places within the house. Be sure to use the words in context rather than simply listing names. Allow children to supplement English terms with their native tongue if necessary to keep the flow of the description going.

13. Ask students to search for letters that represent a particular sound in English. Start with simple sounds, avoiding those that can be made with more than one letter. It's easiest to have students listen for beginning or ending sounds in words. Working in groups, students can cut out other words that begin or end with that letter and paste them on paper. Do not ask for isolated letters; students can highlight target letters by circling them within each word. Display each group's paper to the class and read each word aloud, stressing the target sound. Ask students to repeat the words after you. Then choose a few familiar words from the papers and write them on the blackboard. Enlist students' help to build phrases or sentences with those words. Repeat each phrase or sentence, stressing the sound studied during the lesson.

14. When students unfamiliar with the Latin alphabet used in English have acquired enough of the language to start identifying the order of the letters, ask them to clip the letters out of the newspaper. (For easier manipulation, you can have them paste the letters onto small pieces of construction paper.) Working in small groups, students can

Figure 3
Activity 12: Interior Design

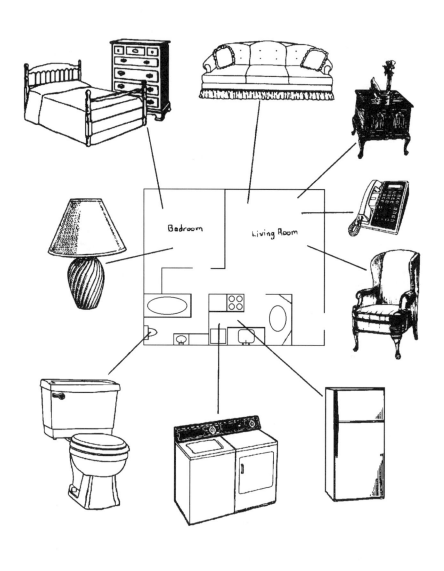

arrange the letters in alphabetical order. After that, they can group the letters by categories such as consonants and vowels, capital and small letters, and so on.

15. In order to learn prepositions of place, students can scan the comics to find pictures that illustrate prepositions called out by the teacher. (For instance, the cat is behind the table; the ball is on the floor.) Use gestures and body language to communicate the meaning of the prepositions. Then ask students to invert the process; working in groups, they can select several cartoon frames that illustrate prepositions, paste them down, and then write sentences for them.

16. To improve comprehension and use of antonyms, have students search the newspaper for words for which they know the opposite—for example, tall/short, small/big, dark/light. Have them make lists of the newspaper words and their opposites. Then ask them to write their words on the blackboard, read them aloud, and make sentences with them.

17. An important skill to develop at the prereading level is the ability to categorize. To work on this skill, ask the students to locate pictures of different types of objects such as foods, clothing, and vehicles in the newspaper. Next have them form groups to cut out the pictures and mount them on tag board by category. In addition to developing categorizing skills, this activity can help LEP students build their vocabularies. If they go on to label each category and the objects in it, students can practice reading and writing as well. (See Figure 4 for an example.) Variations on this activity can be used to extend the lesson. One popular and useful variation is to play matching games with the objects. Students can match pairs of similar pictures, match names with pictures, and so on.

▼ ▼ ▼ ▼ ▼ ▼

Figure 4
Activity 17: Categorizing

18. Divide the class into small groups and give each group a comic strip that has been cut into individual frames. Ask the groups to discuss and decide on the correct sequence of the frames. For beginners, choose a strip with simple text or no text at all. To extend this activity, ask students to describe why they chose that sequence, using whatever language or gestures they want.

19. Ask the students to locate an action photograph in the sports section of the newspaper. Working in groups, they can predict what will happen next. To encourage thinking skills, ask students to explain their predictions.

20. Have each group of students select a different large picture from the paper. See that they choose simple pictures without too many details. Tell them that they will be pretending to describe the picture by telephone to a friend. Each member of the group must learn to describe one aspect of the picture in English. Each group will present its description in front of the class without showing the picture. Then have the class look at the picture and ask the students to comment (in any language) on the problems or omissions in the oral description.

Intermediate/Advanced Activities

1. Ask students to search the newspaper for pictures of clothing that is either in or out of fashion. (The clothing can be depicted by itself— say, in an ad—or on a person.) Have the learners describe whether the clothing is in or out of fashion and why. Ask them to work in small groups to discuss the pros and cons of fashion. Groups can take sides in discussing the issue as a class. After the discussion, students can use a two-column format to write down the pros and cons presented by each group.

2. The food section of a paper can be used to discuss and/or prepare a recipe. Simple recipes can be prepared in the classroom. In talking about the recipes' ingredients, their measurements, and other aspects of preparing food, students will be learning and reinforcing useful vocabulary as well as communicating in a meaningful, context-rich environment.

3. Features or other items about food in the paper can be used to launch a discussion of specific diets such as low fat, no salt, or those for medical conditions such as diabetes. Each group of students can prepare a dish or meal for a different diet and report on the characteristics of the diet and the items allowed under it. These discussions can be expanded to include other aspects of health care or related themes.

4. In groups, students can prepare a complete menu for a special holiday. They should cut out pictures of the food items they want to include and create a visual display for each meal of the day. In honor of the special occasion, students should prepare a sophisticated menu. Each group can then report its selections to the class.

5. For more advanced students, food activities based on the newspaper can be expanded into a complete instructional unit. If the facilities allow it, students can cook and eat more elaborate meals. In addition, they can write and read about particular food items or menus. If the unit involves complex measurements or discussions of nutrition, lessons in mathematics or science can be tied in (see chapter 4).

6. Ask each group to select a large newspaper ad that contains photographs or drawings as well as text. After the group members have studied the ad carefully, have them analyze and discuss the advertiser's intentions and list all the features the ad uses to influence the consumer. Suggest features such as stereotypes, appeals, discounts, type

features (e.g. the size of the word "discount" compared with the size of the actual price), and graphic elements. (Figure 5 gives an example.) Ask each group to write its findings and report to the whole class in a formal presentation.

7. Have groups of students choose an advertisement from the newspaper and then change some of the words in the ad to their opposites. Ask each group to redesign the ad with the antonyms and discuss the new meaning of the ad. When the redesigned ads are displayed, the class can comment on which ones are funny, impossible, or even more honest than the originals!

8. Have students read ads placed by people who are looking for a lost pet. Initiate a discussion about the importance of pets in many countries. Then have groups work together to write lost-pet ads describing group members' pets. Students can also write classified ads for items they wish to sell or buy.

9. Ask students to go through the classified section of the newspaper and choose a help-wanted ad. Working in groups they can discuss the professional qualifications necessary for the job, the personal characteristics that could help or hinder success in that position, and other jobs that require the same or similar qualifications.

10. Students can work in groups to create a hypothetical company. After discussing their personnel needs, they can write help-wanted ads for the newspaper. Ask them to discuss and explain how they chose the items to include in the ad. Then they can take on different roles as each group interviews other groups' members as potential employees.

11. As a complement to the preceding activity, students can learn more about the help-wanted section from the reader's perspective. First divide the class into small groups to dis-

Figure 5
Activity 6: Analyzing Advertising

cuss the meaning of the abbreviations used in that section. Then have them write a letter answering a particular ad.

12. Ask the students to compare the occupations they read about in the newspaper with those they know of in their or their parents' native countries. Ask them to discuss how similar occupations are performed differently in different countries. Ask them to suggest reasons for these differences and report their findings to the class. Then have the class discuss and compare findings.

13. Groups of students can use the maps and other information in the weather section to choose a location for a ski or warm-weather vacation. For a writing exercise, they can describe where their location is and how to get there. A variation of this activity is to create a newspaper ad for the location describing the weather conditions and activities available at this time of the year.

14. Ahead of class time, cut apart the frames of several copies of a comic strip. Be sure to choose a strip with a clear sequence. Then remove one frame from each strip and have students work in groups to put the remaining ones in order, creating their own frame to complete the sequence. As an extension to this activity, ask the students to describe why they chose the sequence they did and how they decided what to include in the missing frame.

15. Have students locate newspaper photos showing people's faces. Working in groups, they can discuss which emotions, if any, are shown by the people in two or three of the pictures. Ask the groups to infer or speculate about why each person might be feeling those emotions. If they are able, they should review the text accompanying the photo to find out something about the person pictured. Each group can prepare a short presentation for the class, showing the pictures, describing each person's emotions, and

speculating about why the people are feeling that way. More advanced students can also describe the thought process behind their speculations.

16. Ask students in groups to find a large newspaper photograph with several elements and cut it out. Have students paste the picture on a large piece of construction paper and use arrows to connect each major element with a sentence describing its position. An example would be "The people are in front of the building." Ask the groups to present their papers to the class with the photograph covered. Class members can describe how they think the picture looks on the basis of the sentences around it. Then uncover the picture and discuss with the students any problems they saw in the communication process.

17. Bring in an editorial cartoon for each group in your class. Ask the students to discuss the meaning of the cartoon. What is the artist trying to say? How does he or she convey meaning? Discuss the use of exaggeration, satire, cultural references, and other elements.

18. Ask students to choose an action shot from the sports section and work in groups to (1) infer what happened just before the picture was taken, and (2) predict what will happen next. Ask them to write sentences or a short paragraph explaining their answers and how they arrived at them. What information did they consider, and what was their thought process?

19. Have students cut out a funny or interesting photo depicting one or more people and paste it on a sheet of construction paper. In groups, they can draw dialogue balloons and write a sentence for each one. Language learning often comes more easily when students get caught up in this kind of fun and creative exercise. Display the results in the classroom for everybody to read and comment on.

20. Read a letter to the editor with the class and discuss the importance of this forum in many cultures. Ask each group of students to choose a controversial social or community issue and write a letter to the editor about it. This activity may take several sessions; when students are satisfied with their letters, they should mail them to the local newspaper.

21. Choose a short article from the newspaper and ask small groups to rewrite it as a news story for a radio station. Have each student audiotape the story and play it back for discussion with the rest of the group. Play one tape from each group for the whole class. Students can discuss how each group approached the story and point to areas where the speaker's pronunciation could be improved. A similar activity is to have students work in groups to adapt a newspaper ad for the radio. Each group should tape the ad, adding music and sound effects if possible, and then play it back for the class.

22. For something a little off-beat, take out a classified ad in the local newspaper to send a special message to your class. If possible, the message could carry some instructions for a classroom activity, along with a greeting. To help students find the message, direct them to the correct page and ask them to review the ads in the column in which your message appears. The surprise will give students extra motivation for the day's activities.

Integrating Language Instruction and the Content Areas

This chapter provides teachers with both a theoretical framework and practical procedures for using the newspaper to integrate language instruction into the content areas. Bilingual and ESL instructors, as well as mainstream teachers who are working with limited English proficient students, will find here descriptions of classroom strategies that will help them improve students' second-language acquisition while teaching concepts in mathematics, science, or social studies.

The chapter opens with an overview of research and theory in this area. The next section discusses classroom organization and environment. The rest of the chapter is devoted to techniques teachers can use to integrate second-language instruction into other subject areas. Specific classroom activities that make use of the newspaper to enhance language and content area learning are presented in chapter 5.

Theory and Research

Over the past three decades, several instructional approaches have been touted as the most effective procedure for teaching English to nonnative speakers. In the 1960s, the behaviorist theories that dominated education introduced second-language teaching to the notions of stimulus-response, habit strength, reinforcement, and practice (Genese, 1991). In keeping with the behaviorist principles of practice makes perfect and the more time on task the better, the audiolingual approach was developed. ESL teachers who practice this approach stress linguistic activities in which stimulus and reinforcement are carefully planned to teach sentence patterns. To create the necessary "selected sentence structures" for this practice, teachers create artificial interactions that simulate real-life dialogues while stressing a particular pattern. The idea is to have students repeat the grammatical structures under review as many times as possible (Lessow-Hurley, 1990).

By definition, structure-oriented approaches entail classroom activities that focus on learning the rules of the second language. Because the emphasis is on grammatical structures and phonics, drill and repetition are the main components of classroom interactions. Both teacher-student and student-student interaction are designed to practice common language patterns (Ovando & Collier, 1985). The content of the message is relatively unimportant.

Because of this focus on structure, the audiolingual approach generally teaches the second language in isolation from other areas of the curriculum. Thus, it tends to delay students' ability to satisfy their requirements in other areas of the curriculum. This poses a serious problem since neither the students nor the school system has time to put off the development of knowledge and cognitive skills in the content areas until the second language has been completely mastered. To meet the academic needs of students—and of the curriculum—bilingual, ESL, and mainstream teachers must integrate second-language and content learning.

In an extensive review of the research on second-language development in school, Genese (1991) confirmed this idea, finding that instructional approaches that isolate language learning from other curriculum subjects tend to be less effective than those that integrate content and language. Numerous others have reached the same conclusion, on the basis of both research and classroom experience (Cochran, 1985; Early, 1990; Sutman, Allen, & Shoemaker, 1986). In the 1980s instructional education writers began to build on this research in recommending classroom strategies and developing instructional materials (De Avila, Duncan, & Navarrete, 1987; Secada, 1989; Short, 1988).

Language theory also supports the idea of teaching a second language within the context of the content areas. LEP students, like other students, need to develop both social and academic language skills. As outlined by Cummins (1981), these students need a language learning environment that will let them develop their basic interpersonal communicative skills as well as their cognitive academic language proficiency. To acquire the latter, they must be exposed to learning situations that are rich in context clues. Subjects such as math, science, and social studies provide a built-in context that can help students acquire language more easily. In addition, because these subject areas are cognitively demanding, they can help students develop thinking skills as well as linguistic proficiency. In fact, a second-language program that integrates language instruction with content area learning "appears to be a particularly promising way to develop simultaneously students' language, subject area knowledge, and thinking skills" (Early, 1990, p. 568).

Using the second language with an academic purpose also facilitates the transition from language acquisition to language learning (Romero, 1991). Thus, it helps students transfer their language skills to new situations. Transference also plays a role when it comes to content knowledge. Students who already understand some of the concepts of a given subject area in their native language can transfer those concepts to the second language; all they have to do is change the labels from one language to the other. For those students, learning a second language within the context of a subject area will be more academically efficient than learning the language in isolation.

Practical considerations also support an integrated approach to language instruction. School time is limited, and LEP students need to develop cognitive skills in the subject areas as well as proficiency in the second language (Mohan, 1986). For students in bilingual classes this need is not as urgent as it is for LEP students attending mainstream classes and receiving some additional ESL instruction. Bilingual classrooms continue reinforcing and developing content area knowledge in the native language while helping students transfer that knowledge to the second language. Students receiving only ESL services are at a disadvantage because they have to learn subject matter in an unfamiliar language. If they are part of a pullout ESL program, chances are they will be losing classroom instruction in the content areas to attend their ESL classes. If the ESL teacher focuses instruction exclusively on language proficiency, students will be left on their own to try to connect the cognitive demands of the subject areas with those of the language instruction. In addition, they have to make up the content learned when they were out attending ESL classes.

An ESL program in which the second-language teacher works with mainstream teachers to integrate math, science, and other subjects into language learning activities sidesteps all of these problems. It provides an academic environment full of context clues, which helps students develop both language skills and content knowledge more effectively. This approach can also improve LEP students' overall performance by encouraging class participation, which in turn boosts self-esteem and stimulates active learning.

▼ ▼ ▼ ▼ ▼

Classroom Organization and Environment

Using the newspaper to teach a second language within the content areas requires a specific type of classroom environment. Research indicates that as with any type of second-language learning, students in an integrated language/content program learn better when they work cooperatively (Levine, 1985). Cooperative learning has a number of benefits for such students. McGroarty (1989) found that the cooperative learning approach increased the frequency and variety of second-language practice through different types of interactions. In addition, working with their peers allows LEP students to make use of their first language in ways that support cognitive development. Since the teacher is not the only source of information, students are in contact with a greater variety of curricular materials and stimuli. This variety stimulates concept learning as well as language use. And since students can use each other as information sources, they take an active role in learning.

In addition to the general guidelines for cooperative learning outlined in chapter 2, some specific issues should be considered when it comes to content area instruction. For example, it is helpful to place at least one native English speaker or an advanced second-language learner in each small group. Heterogeneous grouping will benefit everyone—even more so than in other cooperative learning situations, since in this case both language and content knowledge can be shared. Students with advanced ESL skills will reinforce their own grasp of the concepts being learned while they explain them to others. Meanwhile, the less advanced students will be learning in a context-rich environment that invites participation (with both content and language at issue, everyone will have something to contribute).

However, some precautions are necessary with this kind of classroom organization. Teachers should be careful not to point to advanced ESL students or native English speakers as "helpers" because some students will condescend. Group assignments must be seen as regular work within the content area. As with other cooperative learning assignments, each group member should have an active role that requires performing a specific task. Teachers should also regroup students frequently to avoid letting some students become dependent on others. Finally, the cooperative learning approach should be used in conjunction with other strategies rather than as the only classroom organization (Levine, 1985).

In addition to classroom organization, teachers who want to integrate second-language instruction into the content areas must consider several other aspects of instruction. For example, classroom activities should move from the concrete to the abstract as students become more proficient in the language and more knowledgeable in the subject area. Including a hands-on component is a good idea since hands-on activities provide the LEP learner with context clues that can facilitate later abstractions and conceptualizations (Sutman, Allen, & Shoemaker, 1986). Because newspapers are so easily manipulated, they are ideal for this; most of the newspaper activities presented in the next chapter have some hands-on involvement.

If activities need written instructions, teachers should use short, fairly simple sentences. Students can be taught to prepare outlines for prereading and prewriting activities to make sure they understand what is expected of them. To ensure that students learn the content area lesson, it is important to minimize any obstacles to learning created by language interference. At the same time, teachers should avoid planning simplistic activities that demand only recollection or arrangement of information. The best strategies in this regard are those that emphasize learning to have control over information rather than simply learning facts (Driver, 1979).

To explain complex concepts in a content area, teachers should use any means of communication necessary, including gestures, body language, photographs, drawings, or the students' native language. To make sure students understand important vocabulary, teachers must decide in advance which key terms might need special explanation and how they can get the idea across using only known words.

When asking students to answer questions or give explanations orally, teachers should attend to what the students are saying rather than to how they're saying it (Chamot & Arambul, 1985). Interrupting the message to correct a language error will discourage students from participating and remove the focus from how well they are mastering the content. Teachers should also be aware that they should not try to speed up groups or individuals who are working to the best of their ability. Language and content accuracy are more important than speed.

Finally, to stress the language component of the lesson, teachers can provide homework that involves a number of second-language skills as well as content area knowledge. Completed assignments should be displayed in the classroom; later, the teacher can return to the displays to reinforce different aspects of the lesson.

Integration Techniques

Several classroom strategies can be used to facilitate the integration of second-language learning into content area instruction. These techniques can help reinforce a lesson's language skills, content area information, or both. Of course, these techniques should not be used exclusively; however, when chosen carefully and used in conjunction with other approaches, they can enhance learning among LEP students.

Semantic Maps

Semantic maps can help teachers develop and expand students' content vocabularies as well as introduce or reinforce language structures. Johnson (1981) applied the concept of the semantic map to a vocabulary-building technique derived from flow charts that show the relationship between blocks. Semantic maps, also known as semantic networks, semantic webs, or plot maps (Rodriguez, 1986), chart the connections among semantically related words. Known words, along with new words being introduced in the lesson, are arranged in categories and connected graphically. For example, if the class is reading a newspaper article on rain forests for a science lesson, the students can map new terms encountered (such as *greenhouse* or *arachnids*) and familiar words (such as *food* and *hot*) to show their relationship to rain forests. Students should provide these words, either from the reading or from their own knowledge. At first, have them simply connect the term *rain forest* with words that are directly or indirectly related. The resulting map will look like a web (Figure 6). Later these words can be organized into categories.

A semantic map does more than provide spellings of and semantic links between new and known words. Because words are given context by their relationship to each other and by their position within categories, semantic maps also help reading comprehension and thinking skills.

Semantic maps are a good way to introduce new vocabulary to second-language learners. Since the context arises from the logical connections among words, there is no need for a more complex syntactical structure to provide meaning. For a prereading activity, students can build semantic maps using any kind of communication. They can draw, clip pictures from the newspaper, gesture, or use their native language when necessary. Teachers can use similar techniques to explain in detail the relationships among words. If semantic maps are used during or after reading, more emphasis can be placed on writing words correctly.

Creating a semantic map helps students develop and reinforce thinking skills such as categorizing, classifying, organizing, and selecting. At the same time, the decision-making process involved

Figure 6
Semantic Map: First Step

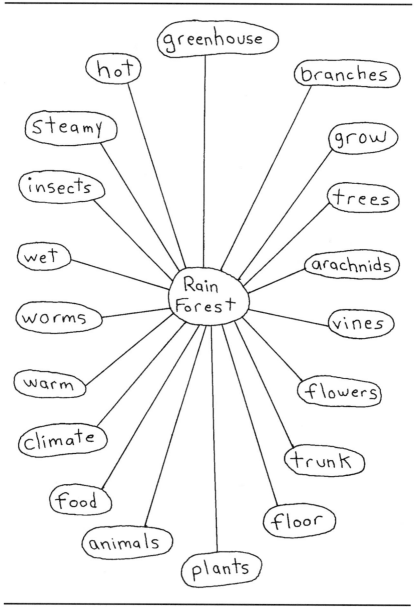

greenhouse

hot

branches

steamy

grow

insects

trees

wet

arachnids

Rain
Forest

worms

vines

warm

flowers

climate

trunk

food

floor

animals

plants

can boost LEP students' confidence and help them develop their sense of self. Since semantic mapping calls for students to draw on their personal experiences to make associations, their cultural backgrounds can be of use—and thus a source of pride rather than embarrassment.

The following steps outline the general procedure for guiding students in creating a semantic map:

1. Ask the class to choose one of the terms that came up often in the last exercise with the newspaper.

2. Write the word on the blackboard. Divide the students into small groups and ask each group to write the word in the center of a large piece of paper.

3. Have students work together to provide as many words as possible that they think are related to the central word. Beginners can cut out pictures representing words; advanced and intermediate students can write words on small pieces of paper.

4. Ask students to group the related words into categories, with a name for each category. If a word falls into more than one category, it should be repeated as many times as possible.

5. Have students paste or write their categorized words around the central term.

6. Display each group's semantic map and ask its members to describe their work.

7. Create a big semantic map that integrates the work of all the groups in the class. The completed map will look something like the one in Figure 7.

8. Discuss the words chosen, their connection with the other words in the category, and their relationship to the central term.

Figure 7
Semantic Map: Final Step

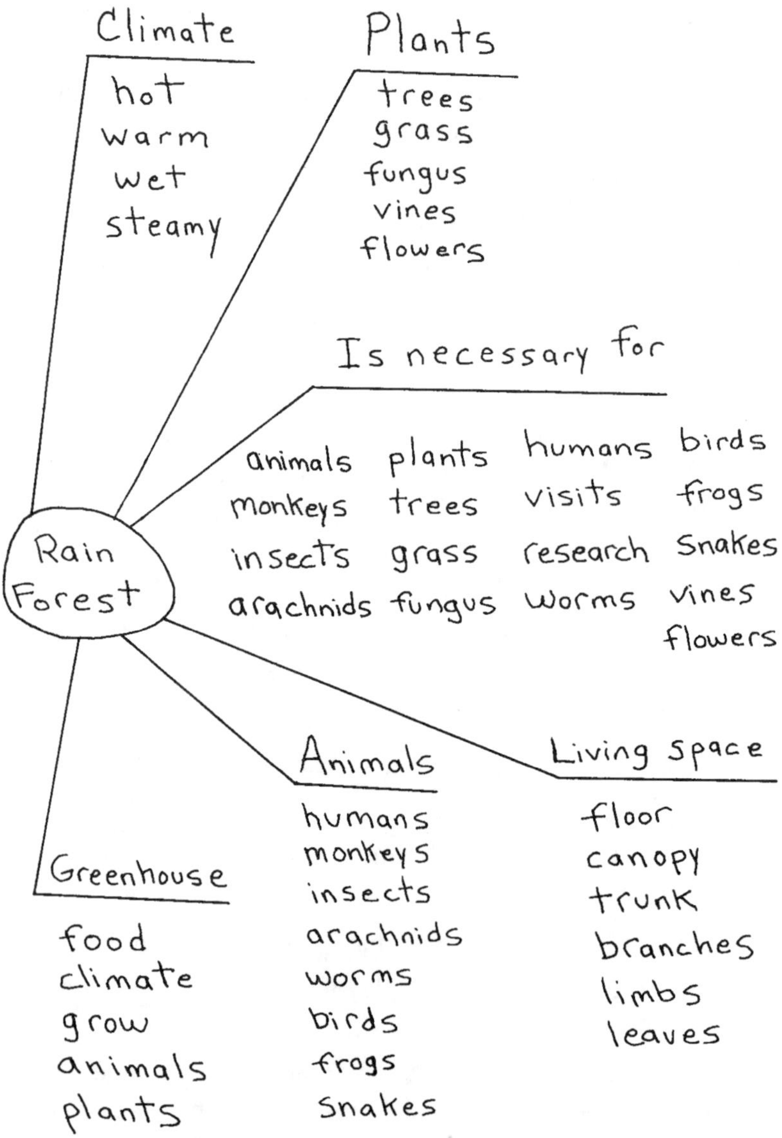

Climate
hot
warm
wet
steamy

Plants
trees
grass
fungus
vines
flowers

Is necessary for

animals   plants   humans   birds
monkeys   trees   visits   frogs
insects   grass   research snakes
arachnids fungus   worms   vines
                            flowers

Rain Forest

Animals
humans
monkeys
insects
arachnids
worms
birds
frogs
snakes

Living space
floor
canopy
trunk
branches
limbs
leaves

Greenhouse
food
climate
grow
animals
plants

Concept Maps

Concept maps are another practical technique that can help teachers link second-language learning and content area instruction. The idea is to organize the concepts, terms, and words used into a diagram that depicts the relationships among those concepts. The diagram can be designed as a tree with branches or as a flowchart. Branches of the map can list concepts in a sequence or in some other kind of order or categorization.

To guide LEP students in creating and elaborating on a concept map, teachers can follow three steps:

1. Ask students to list the key words and concepts used during a lesson.

2. Recommend or have students propose a hierarchy for the concepts. One arrangement is to begin with the broadest concept and end with the smallest, following a deductive sequence. If the subject under study allows it, the concepts can also be arranged in an inductive sequence. Cause and effect, chronology, or other sequencing patterns can also be used. If more than one sequence exists, the concept map can have several branches (see Figure 8).

3. Have students write the concepts on the blackboard or on a large piece of paper, drawing lines or arrows to join the related concepts. To make the connection among concepts clear, words can be added between them to make full phrases or sentences.

School subjects such as math, science, and social studies introduce students to specific, often unfamiliar, concepts. Concept mapping can help all learners better understand new concepts and reinforce the ones they already know. In addition, since this technique focuses on meaning but also offers guidance in spelling and structure, it will help LEP students with both language acquisition and language learning.

Figure 8
Concept Map for a Lesson on Health

Procedure
- List the concepts: balanced diet, junk food, vegetables, fruits, meat, milk, grains, exercise, sports, baseball, drinking, person, potato chips, soccer, smoking, health, candy, walking, dancing, body
- Arrange concepts in one or more hierarchies:
  (a) Person, health, balanced diet, fruits, vegetables, grains, meat, milk, exercise, sports, baseball, soccer, walking, dancing, body
  (b) Person, junk food, potato chips, candy, smoking, drinking, body
- Draw a diagram of the concepts adding connecting words as necessary.

Although concept maps can look very similar to semantic maps, there are some fundamental differences. The words on a semantic map are linked only by their direct or indirect association with the main term. Because semantic maps are based on the meanings of the individual words, they are more linguistically than conceptually oriented. In contrast, the terms on a concept map are linked by their conceptual relationship to the topic under study. The semantics of the terminology is important only in making explicit relationships among specific terms in the sequence.

Since concept maps are more content than linguistically oriented, they can help LEP students assimilate the concepts introduced in a content area lesson and place them within a conceptual hierarchy. This in turn helps them internalize the entire conceptual system. At the same time, the structure of the concept map draws grammatical, sequential, and conceptual links among the terms used. Working out those relationships helps LEP students develop their thinking skills in the areas of representation and elaboration (Langrehr, 1988). In deciding on the organization of the concept map, students must exercise their ability to work with abstractions. Before they can draw their diagram, they have to compare, categorize, and choose a sequence for the concepts. In order to link the concepts graphically and to add the appropriate connector words, they must understand and elaborate on the relationships among all of the diagram's concepts. In doing so, the students will be using prior knowledge to give meaning to new information. This, of course, is the way to develop high-level cognitive skills.

Other Techniques

In addition to semantic maps and concept maps, a number of other techniques can be used to highlight the second-language component in a content area lesson. Two particularly effective methods that work well in conjunction with the newspaper are crossword puzzles and forced combinations.

Crossword puzzles. Creating or solving a crossword puzzle with words and concepts drawn from a specific content area lesson can help LEP students improve both their language skills and their knowledge of the subject under study. In order to have meaning, the sentences and phrases in a crossword puzzle have to provide conceptual and/or semantic clues. These clues put the second-language words into context, which aids in language acquisition and conceptual understanding. Crossword puzzles also facilitate language learning by forcing students to attend to language structures and spelling (spelling mistakes become apparent quickly in a crossword).

One popular activity is to have small groups of students use the terminology of a content area lesson to create a puzzle. Groups can exchange puzzles for solving and then discuss how they developed the crosswords and clues. Teachers can display the completed puzzles or select the best few and maintain a bank of puzzles for future lessons. To expand on this activity, teachers can have students work with software that helps users construct crossword puzzles.

For either student-made or teacher-made puzzles, it is important to remember these guidelines:

- Puzzle clues should always contain clear definitions or synonyms.
- Clues and answers should be taken from a limited pool. Words taken from more than one or two lessons can make the puzzles so difficult that it will frustrate the solver.
- Easy and difficult words should be combined in the puzzles and in the clues. The overall degree of difficulty should be carefully adjusted according to the language proficiency of the students.
- It's a good idea to provide a list of words containing the answers to the puzzle. The length of the list and the terms

included can vary with the students' language proficiency. Students can use the list to get hints if they become stuck.

Keep in mind that crossword puzzles offer an ideal opportunity to individualize instruction. Students can work by themselves or in pairs to create or solve a puzzle at their own level while the rest of the class is working on other activities.

Forced combinations. Forced combinations is an interesting technique that allows advanced LEP students to break away from traditional word combinations and create inventive combinations of their own. The various activities derived from forced combinations can not only stimulate learning in the second language and reinforce concepts in the content area but also help students develop thinking skills (Langrehr, 1990).

To use forced combinations, have students choose an object that came up during the last lesson. For example, after a social studies lesson during which students read and discussed a newspaper article on communication, they might choose the telephone. Once they have chosen an object, help them select two or three categories of characteristics (e.g., "source of power"). Then have them brainstorm to list the attributes the object can have within those categories. Arrange the categories in columns on the chalkboard. (Students can do the same at their desks.) The result will look something like this:

Telephone

Material	Type of Power	Transmission
plastic	electric	wire
steel	battery	fiber-optic cable
wood	solar	computer
fiberglass	magnetic	radio waves

Groups of students can then choose one word from each column to use in a sentence about telephones. Typical sentences might include "In the future all phones might be made of fiberglass, powered by solar energy, and have fiber-optic transmission" or "My cordless phone is made of plastic and uses electric power to carry signals."

The combinations that arise from these connections will spur discussion about the content of the lesson as well as about vocabulary and sentence construction. These interactive situations will let students practice all their language skills.

LEP students who do not yet write proficiently can work in forced combinations by cutting and pasting objects from the newspaper. For example, they might arrange different kinds of foods into columns. Using oral communication they can create different dishes and combinations of foods.

All forced combinations require students to produce language. They have to discuss combinations, exploring plausible ones and discarding silly or impossible ones. In discussing and making decisions about combinations, students are engaging in the kind of context-rich conversation that helps develop language skills and content knowledge (as well as decision-making skills).

Extension activities. After working with semantic maps, concept maps, crossword puzzles, or forced combinations, students will have a collection of connected phrases or sentences and many related words. Teachers can use these words and sentences in any number of ways to further develop skill in the second language. For instance, groups of students can write paragraphs combining related words and sentences and then analyze the paragraphs semantically and structurally. Afterwards, they can transform the paragraphs of other groups by introducing new words that change the meaning.

Using these techniques, the possibilities for classroom activities are virtually limitless. Teachers must keep two important caveats in mind, however. First, no matter what exercise is suggested, be sure to keep the communication within a familiar context. Don't let the conversation stray from the theme, particularly if it means exposing students to unknown concepts and terminology. Introducing new vocabulary when students are still practicing terms they've recently acquired can cause confusion.

Second, when students are engaged in oral or written communication, keep the flow going by allowing structural or grammatical errors to pass. Of course, teachers should always provide an example by using proper language structures, but LEP students should be allowed to internalize those structures in the normal course of acquiring and learning the second language.

Classroom Activities in the Content Areas

Because the activities presented in this chapter are arranged to take advantage of different features of the newspaper, they do not represent a logical curriculum sequence; it is up to the teacher to decide when and how to use each activity, based on students' proficiency in the second language and their ability to work with the concepts and processes involved in the activity. To facilitate such decisions, each section has been divided into two levels: activities for students with a low level of English proficiency (beginning) and activities for those with more developed English proficiency (intermediate/advanced). Since most of the activities encompass more than one concept or skill, teachers must decide which aspect or aspects to emphasize to best meet their students' needs.

Mathematics

The newspaper offers numerous opportunities to study mathematical concepts in the context of real-life situations. By computing salaries, budgets, measurement, and other data using information in the newspaper, students can acquire skill in arithmetic, fractions, percentages, and other mathematical functions.

A good follow-up to any of the activities in this section is to have groups of students create and trade word problems involving the topic or function being studied. This strategy provides a perfect blend of language practice (in both reading and writing) and content learning.

Beginning Activities

1. Ask students to cut out photographs, drawings, or advertisements in the newspaper that represent sets of 1, 2, 3, and so on through 10. (These sets should consist of the particular number of items pictured rather than actual numerals.) Then have students paste their sets onto construction paper or poster board and label them. If necessary, they can use their native language to identify the sets; the teacher can help them with the English labels. (See Figure 9.) Using both languages can help students understand that the concept represented in each set goes beyond the linguistic label. Completed number sets can be saved for future exercises.

2. For a slightly more advanced activity, ask students to search the newspaper for numerals of any size and then cut out and paste the numerals onto a large piece of construction paper. Working cooperatively in small groups, students can write the name of each number next to the numeral. Have each group describe its work to the class, pointing to and stating the name of each numeral. Encourage the students who are least proficient in English to present the report. If necessary, the other members of the group can coach the reporter.

3. After the students are able to recognize the names of

Figure 9
Activity 1: Number Sets

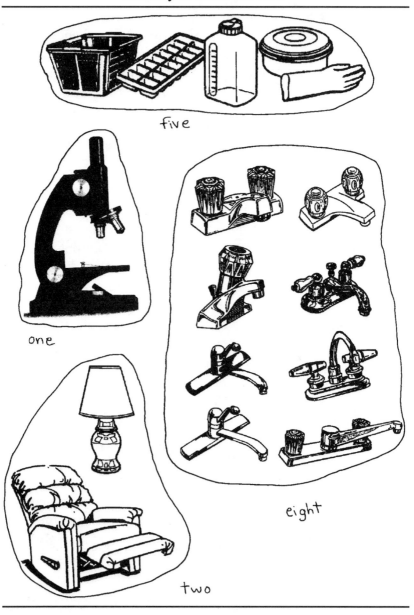

five

one

eight

two

numerals, have them work in groups to clip spelled-out numbers from the newspaper and paste them on a sheet. Ask them to write the corresponding numeral next to each word. Then have them fill in some of the gaps between numbers, consulting with others in their group as needed. As a follow-up, have students compare the number of letters in the word for the largest number found with the length of the numeral. Comparisons can also be made between how large numbers are read in the United States and how they are read in other countries. Example: 1,000,000,000 is called one billion in the United States but one thousand million in South America.

4. Ask students to cut out all the numerals they can find in the newspaper. Have them work in groups to arrange the numbers in sequence on construction paper, leaving space between nonconsecutive numbers so they can fill in the missing ones by hand. (Example: 6...35...100...720...1200) To avoid long lists, students can fill the first part of each gap with individual units until they reach a multiple of 10. After that, they can use tens, hundreds, or thousands until they reach the next cut-out numeral. The purpose of the exercise is to maintain a sequence with the least number of numerals. For the example above, the blanks will be filled as follows: 1, 2, 3, 4, 5, *6,* 7, 8, 9, 10, 20, 30, *35,* 36, 37, 38, 39, 40, 50, 60, 70, 80, 90, *100,* 200, 300, 400, 500, 600, 700, *720,* 730, 740, 750, 760, 770, 780, 790, 800, 900, 1000, *1200.* Each member of the group should be able to read any number on the list. Students who need help can be coached by peers in the group. Allow the students to use their native language if necessary to explain the instructions.

5. To help students learn to compare sizes, ask them to identify the largest and smallest items in a photo or a drawing.

(The concepts of tallest and shortest can also be introduced here.) In groups, have students record the names of the items and write sentences that describe each one.

6. To learn the English names for various geometric shapes, students can work in groups to cut out all the logos they can find in a newspaper. Ask them to arrange the logos in groups according to the geometric shape they most closely resemble (for example, the Mercedes logo would go under circles; the Delta Airlines logo, under triangles). Then have them paste and label the shapes on construction paper. Each member of the group must be able to name all the shapes represented by the logos.

7. Have students review the car ads in the classified section to find the most expensive car listed that day, cars that cost between $1,000 and $1500, the least expensive car listed, and so on. Students can cut out these ads and arrange them in categories according to price. Students can make use of L1 to discuss the categories, but they must use L2 to report their findings to the class. Those who need coaching for the oral presentation can turn to their peers or the teacher.

8. Ask students to scan the ads in the travel section of the newspaper for a trip to an assigned location or to their own or their parents' native country. Working in groups, they can calculate how much the trip will cost for the group or for a family. For an extension activity, have the groups create charts that list the amenities offered by each company, along with the price for each travel package. Students can discuss and compare the various options to determine the best value.

9. To give students practice calculating percentages and to help them gain some insight into the cost of living, have groups search the newspaper ads for a full outfit. They can look for shirts, pants, dresses, skirts, coats, socks, shoes,

and other articles of clothing. Ask them to calculate the full cost of the outfit, then the cost with a 10 or 20 percent discount. They can also add in sales tax, if applicable. While they work, they can cut and paste the items, writing in the name and price of each. Or, if their language proficiency allows, they can write out the whole word problem.

10. The classic word problem involving shopping in the supermarket can be practiced with real prices and real products from the newspaper. Ask groups of students to discuss which items from the food section they want to buy for a class party. Have them calculate quantities and prices. To facilitate the interaction in English, students can create charts showing the items, the quantities, and the prices. Then they can figure out the total—with or without taxes.

11. Divide the class into small groups and tell each group that it will have $50 to spend in the supermarket. Ask the groups to simulate a trip to the supermarket and, using the food section of the newspaper as a guide, shop for enough items to feed a family of four for one day. They should calculate the total price of their purchases and the change they'll get back. If you want, have them extrapolate from their one-day figure to compute the cost of groceries for a week, a month, or a year. Allow the students to use any means of communication as they discuss the problem, but have them practice the second language by writing a report about their shopping trip and describing to the class their rationale for buying what they did.

Intermediate/Advanced Activities

1. Students can search the newspaper for numbers written as words or as numerals. Ask them to cut out those numbers along with surrounding context. Have them examine the context to classify the numbers according to the way they

are used—e.g., to express length, time, weight, money, or order (first, second, third). Students can then paste the numbers into columns by use. Discuss with the students some of the peculiarities in how numbers are written in English. Compare features such as capitalization, the order of months and days, how time is expressed, and the linking of words in large numbers in English and in the students' native language.

2. As a follow-up activity, discuss the measurement systems used in different countries. For example, students in American classrooms can use the values found in the previous exercise to convert metric notations to the English system or vice versa. The group work in this exercise will provide students with an opportunity to trade knowledge: the LEP students in the room can frequently offer input about the concepts of the metric system; in exchange they will acquire the language necessary to express those concepts in terms familiar to students more used to the system of measurement used in the U.S.

3. A good exercise for students who need to learn a new system of measurement is to have them find a simple recipe in the food section and convert the measurements from English to metric or vice versa. If you're bold, you can have the groups test their conversions by preparing the recipe with the different measurements.

4. To practice mathematical computations in a practical context, groups of students can search the help-wanted section for a job listing that includes the salary. If the ad gives an annual figure, ask students to calculate the weekly salary. If the ad lists a weekly figure, have them calculate the yearly salary. (See Figure 10 for two possibilities.) Choose different problems for each group. Allow students to use any language while they work, but have each group give

an oral report in English. Encourage the least proficient students to present the reports; the rest of the group can coach them.

5. To teach estimating skills, ask students to estimate the measurements of several parts of a newspaper; for example, they can estimate the length and width of a column, the area of an advertisement, and so on. Then have them measure those items and compare their estimates with the actual measurements. (If the LEP students in U.S. classrooms are more familiar with metric, let them use that system, and take the opportunity to introduce conversions between metric measurements and U.S. measurements.) When each group has made several comparisons, have the students report their findings, including the most and least accurate estimates. For a follow-up activity, you can ask students to estimate and confirm larger measurements— for instance, how many newspaper pages it takes to make up the length of the classroom.

6. Select several short articles with accompanying photographs, graphics, or drawings from different sections of the newspaper and make a copy of the set for each group of students. They can rearrange the elements and try different layouts to compose a pleasing page. If there is a photocopier available, they can enlarge or reduce different elements to achieve a better fit. Be sure the groups read and discuss the content so they can make sensible decisions about their layout. As a final activity they can present their page to the class, explaining the rationale for the design.

7. Ask students to look in the newspaper for advertisements that offer discounts. Have them cut out the ads and arrange them into sets according to the percentage of the discount. Have them pay particular attention to the way the ad is

Figure 10
Activity 4: Computing Salaries

Sales Representative

($35,000 BASE)————— ✶ = $673
a week

National service corp is looking for a highly motivated energetic individ for its home office. This aggressive self-starter must have a 4 yr. degree & proven sales exp.

We offer an excel base salary + an outstanding unlimited commission plan & performance incentive plans. Paid expenses & excel growth oppty to qualified individ.

Those with superior sales abilities interested in becoming part of a successful, quality oriented, & growing national organization should send their resume & salary history to: Selling Unlimited, 100 Sales Street

EOE M/F

TELEPHONE CLERK

Large asset management firm seeks telephone clerk for trading/research departments. Duties include handling incoming and outgoing calls, creating automated rolodex system and other related clerical duties. Hours 8:30 AM-4:30 PM, possible occasional overtime. Salary ($435/week) plus excellent benefit package. Send resume to: Assets Inc., 10 Office Road

✶ = $22,620
a year

worded—for instance, "Up to 20 percent off," "Save 10-30 percent," "One-third off," and so on. Discuss the meaning of each form of discount. Then ask students to calculate prices with and without the discount (have them include tax if you wish). An ideal extension activity is to have students work in groups to create simple problems involving discounts. Each group can write one problem using the information in a newspaper ad and then pass the problem to another group to solve. As noted earlier, this strategy can be very beneficial and should be used as often as possible.

8. Have groups of students find a detailed description of a house or apartment in the real-estate section and, using a ruler and compass, draw a floor plan for how they think the dwelling looks. (It helps to provide students with a sample floor plan; these sometimes appear in the paper, or they can be obtained from a local real-estate agent.) Each room of the plan should include labels and measurements. As an extension activity, have students discuss the features of their dwelling (e.g., number of rooms, closeness to public transportation, garage) and their relative value. Allow students to use any means of communication necessary to provide meaning to the discussion.

9. Students can select a travel advertisement to plan a trip to a country they have heard about. (LEP students may want to choose the country where they or their parents were born.) They can use the information from the paper to prepare a budget that includes airfare, hotel, meals, ground transportation, and other expenses. As a follow-up, have students look in the business section of the paper for the value of the currency in their destination country. Using that information, they can calculate how much money their trip will cost in local currency.

10. Ask students to choose a travel destination from the places advertised in the newspaper. Then have them locate their destination on a map and calculate the distance they'll need to travel to get there. Finally, have them divide the plane or bus fare advertised by the distance to be covered to figure out how much they would be paying per mile or kilometer of travel. If students know or are able to estimate travel times, they can also calculate the cost per minute or hour of travel.

11. Ask students to cut out numbers from the newspaper and arrange them in different categories: whole numbers, negative numbers, common fractions, decimal fractions, etc. They can work in groups to order the numbers in each category according to value. Ask them to write the name of the number (or the numeral, if the original is written out) and to explain the relative values of the numbers. This is a good way to clarify how fractions and negative numbers work.

12. To help students understand the graphic representation of numerical data, ask them to follow the weather section for several days and keep a record of the temperatures in two or three major cities. When they have enough data, ask them to create a graphic (e.g., a chart or a line graph) for each city. (Figure 11 gives an example.) Have groups compare graphics and state the similarities and differences. To extend the activity, have students calculate the average temperature in their cities for the period of time recorded.

13. Ask students to review an article in the paper and count the number of times certain words appear. Use some words students already know, along with two or three new words that the article repeats several times. Ask students to draw a bar graph indicating the number of times each word is repeated. This activity can be extended to include

Figure 11
Activity 12: Temperatures for Miami Beach, Florida, and Fargo, North Dakota, from January 11-17, 1993

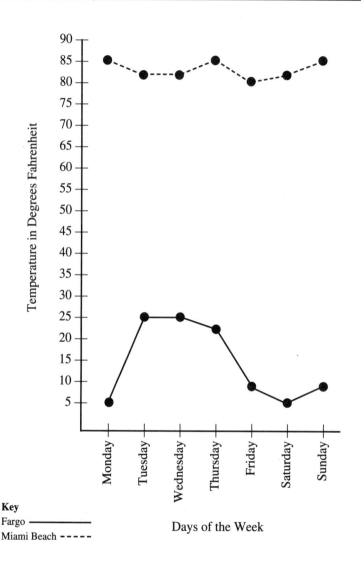

Key
Fargo ——————
Miami Beach - - - - -

other types of graphics by changing what is measured. For example, students can create a line graph that charts how many words have a given number of letters or a pie chart showing the percentage of words with one, two, three, or four syllables. In each of these activities, the words being charted should be written and read aloud.

14. In order to organize data from a primary source, have LEP students and native English speakers work together in groups to review the used-car ads and classify the cars listed according to age, price, or make. With that information they can create graphs to show the most common brands for sale, the number of cars in each price range, or the age ranges of the cars listed. (See Figure 12 for an example.) The groups can also use calculators to compute the average age of all the cars for sale, the average price by brand, and other information.

15. The newspaper is a good resource for developing all kinds of computational games. One fun game is to tell each small group of students that it can "spend" $5,000 using five blank checks (these should be prepared in advance). The groups can expend those checks on any objects or services offered in the paper. The rules of the game are as follows:

  • Each group can use only five checks; the checks can be for any amount as long as they don't add up to more than $5,000.
  • Each group must cut out advertisements with prices for the goods or services they want to buy; the ads should be clipped to each check.
  • The group whose total comes nearest to $5,000 wins.

To facilitate the game and require more reading and writing in English, have students complete the following chart:

Figure 12
**Activity 14: Cars Advertised for Sale in New York City
on January 18, 1993**

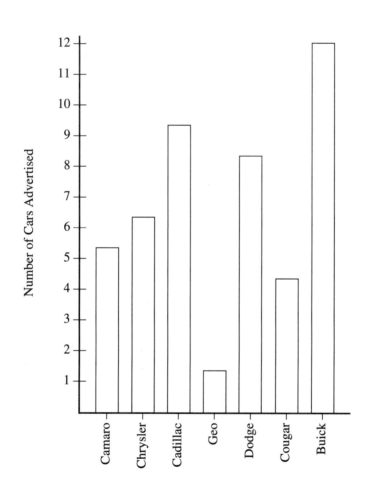

▼ ▼ ▼ ▼ ▼ ▼

Check #	Used for	Amount	Subtotal
1	_____	_____	_____
2	_____	_____	_____
3	_____	_____	_____
4	_____	_____	_____
5	_____	_____	_____
		Total Spent:	_____

16. To practice computation (with or without a calculator) as well as reading in English and problem-solving skills, students can hunt through the newspaper to find items such as these:

- The largest number published in a particular issue
- Any numbers between 2 x (30÷4) and 48 + 16 - 30
- The ratio of the number of news articles to photographs
- The ratio of the number of news articles to advertisements
- A number that is equal to $\dfrac{(5 \times 6) + 3^2}{3}$
- A number that is equal to $\dfrac{(5 \times 8) + 12 - (3 \times 4)}{2 \times 4}$
- All the common fractions that appear in an issue (if desired, students can rewrite them as decimal fractions and in English words)
- All the decimal fractions that appear in an issue (students can rewrite these as common fractions and in words)

- The area of each photo that appears in the sports section
- The approximate area dedicated to news, feature stories, and advertisements

Science

Developing second-language skills through science lessons is a popular approach in ESL and bilingual education because science offers hands-on experiences in which work in small groups—the ideal setup for LEP students—is not only desirable but necessary. The science activities that follow have been created to comply with the methodological recommendations presented in chapters 2 and 4. Most of the activities include one or more of the techniques discussed earlier for integrating second-language and content learning.

An interesting advantage offered by science activities that make use of the newspaper is that they do not require laboratory installations. In fact, all of the activities that follow can be conducted in a regular classroom. Thus, lessons that introduce or reinforce science concepts for LEP students do not necessarily require a special schedule.

Beginning Activities

1. A good activity for the earliest beginning LEP students is to have groups look through the household ads and cut out pictures of a variety of products. With a mixture of English, gestures, and other means of communication, tell students that they are to place their pictures in the first column of a chart you have provided. The other columns of the chart should list the five senses. Have students check off the senses that can be used to recognize the product. (Figure 13 provides an example.) Use English to explain the chart and describe the actions involved in the activity,

but be sure to create a situation full of context clues to help students understand your meaning.

2. In order to develop classification skills, students can scan the newspaper and cut out objects that originated from living things (e.g., a steak), from nonliving things (e.g., a computer), or from a mixture of both (e.g., a bed with a wooden frame). After students have classified their objects, they can create a semantic or concept map. This activity can also lead to some interesting forced combinations (see chapter 4).

3. Ask students to search in the newspaper for all the objects they can find that might be classified as minerals, vegetables, or animals. Then have them go through their objects and select those that clearly belong to one of those classes. In a second review, they can extend the search to objects that originated from one of those classes (e.g., glass). In a third review, they can create a fourth class for objects that are of mixed origin (e.g., salted pretzels, leather furniture). Ask the students to say something about each of the objects and the classes.

4. Have students hunt for photographs and drawings of machines and then cut out and arrange those machines in categories. They can choose any classification scheme they wish. For example, they may classify the machines according to function (transportation, entertainment, household use); type of power (gas, battery, electric); or location of use (indoors/outdoors, urban/rural areas). Have groups paste their pictures on construction paper by category, along with the name of each machine, the name and the attributes of each class, and a general description of the classification scheme.

5. To familiarize students with more scientific classification techniques, ask them to cut out newspaper pictures of liv-

Figure 13
Activity 1: Making Sense of the Senses

Products	We can see it	We can smell it	We can taste it	We can hear it	We can feel it
	✓	✓	✓		✓
	✓			✓	✓
	✓	✓	✓		✓

ing things—either animals or plants. Then have them arrange and paste down the pictures by class, providing instruction as necessary. For animals, for example, they would divide the pictures into mammals, fish, birds, reptiles, insects, etc. They should label each animal and list the attributes of each class. For a more advanced lesson, include other levels of classification, such as order, family, genus, and species.

6. Ask students to work in groups to label the attributes (e.g., gills, beaks, fur, scales) of two or three types of animals whose pictures they cut from the newspaper. Group discussions can be in any language, but the labels should be in English. Have the groups paste each animal in the center of a large piece of construction paper and write the attributes around it in the appropriate places. Then ask each group to present its work to the rest of the class. Presentations should be made by the students with the least proficiency in L2; other group members can provide encouragement and coaching. If desired, repeat this activity with plants found in illustrations in the newspaper.

7. Ask groups of students to find as many items as they can in the newspaper that have to do with staying in good health. Items can include healthy foods, medicines, exercise equipment, sports gear, and people exercising or playing sports. Ask them to paste these items around the word "Healthy" on a piece of construction paper to create a concept map. Students can use these maps to propose the connection between health and the various aspects of diet, exercise, and other factors pictured. Ask the groups to draw additional connections using vocabulary they already know. Each group can then show its map to the class and explain the connections. If you want, have students copy each map in their notebooks, substituting words for pictures.

8. In order to stress the idea of proper nutrition, have students cut out examples of healthy and unhealthy food from the supermarket ads. Students can then pin their examples in turn on two big posters labeled something like "Junk Food Mary" and "Healthy Food Jeanne." As each student goes up, he or she must provide the rationale for the item's placement. Words used in this activity can be written down and used later to create a semantic map.

9. Ask students to work in groups to plan a balanced meal. Each group should work on a different type of meal: breakfast, lunch, supper, formal dinner, picnic, classroom party, snack for a trip, and so on. Students can cut, paste, and label foods advertised in the newspaper to make up their assigned meal. Ask each group to report its plan to the class, stressing how its meal makes up part of a balanced diet. As in other activities, students with low oral proficiency should present the report, with other group members acting as coaches.

10. To extend the previous activity, have students plan an entire week's menu using items clipped from the paper. Discuss the importance of providing balanced meals to make up a healthy overall diet. Have students write down the names of all of the foods by category and then create a semantic or concept map.

Intermediate/Advanced Activities

1. Ask the students to search for news of some natural phenomenon that became a catastrophe for humans, such as an earthquake, flood, or hurricane. They should read the article in small groups and comment on the facts reported. Then have them copy one sentence that describes each of the following: facts about the phenomenon, attitudes of the affected population, and declarations of the authorities.

Using information from the article or their own knowledge, they can create two or three additional sentences on each topic to flesh out or clarify the first sentence. Finally, ask students to use their background knowledge or information from their science reading to discuss the possible causes of the catastrophe.

2. Ask students to review a major urban newspaper for one week and make note of all the deaths reported in the news (as opposed to the obituaries). With that information students can work in groups to list the deaths reported and their causes (for example, natural disasters, disease, accidents, crime, drugs, or natural causes). The lists should include information about each person's age, sex, ethnicity, and neighborhood, as well as other data reported by the paper. Have students organize the information on charts or graphs. After discussing their findings in small groups, they can write a report describing what they think about the outcome of their research.

3. To help students understand the difference between scientific and aesthetic opinions, have them find pictures in the newspaper of things they consider beautiful. Ask them to work in groups to paste these things on the top half of a large piece of construction paper. On the bottom half have them paste pictures of things that they know other people consider beautiful. Ask them to discuss (in any language) these questions: What makes them think the things they have chosen are beautiful? Why do they think other people appreciate the other things? What is the rationale for these kinds of judgments? How does this differ from judgments about things that can be measured and quantified? This activity has the added benefit of helping students understand the validity of diverse opinions.

▼ ▼ ▼ ▼ ▼

4. Ask students to work in groups to find and discuss an easy recipe from the newspaper. The recipe should be simple to prepare (no cooking) and healthy to eat. Once each group has a recipe, you can assign a number of exercises that combine science, math, and language learning. For instance, have students rewrite the recipe to serve one-third the number of people, or ask them to analyze the ingredients for nutritional value. If you want, you can take the opportunity to discuss what happens when different substances are combined. For a later lesson, groups can bring the ingredients for their recipes, and the class can share a meal. During the meal, each group can report on the nutritional value of its recipe.

5. Ask students to work in groups to study the weather maps and charts in the newspaper. Ask them to discuss why different regions have different weather patterns. Have them write or present oral reports on the weather conditions in a particular area. As an extension activity, have them compare the weather where they are now with the weather in their or their parents' native country.

6. Have students work in small groups to find a newspaper article about a scientific discovery or research project. Ask them to read the article and discuss it until each member of the group is able to present the main idea and some supporting details. Allow the use of any means of communication during the discussion, but make sure that in the end all students understand the concepts and vocabulary in English. If applicable, each group can create diagrams or drawings to explain the facts presented in the article. Afterwards, the whole class can work together to formulate a semantic or concept map using the most important words from the article.

7. Many newspapers have a weekly science or technology section that includes information about personalities in the world of science. Have small groups of students read about one such person and coach each other until every group member is able to report on the main points discussed in the article. Have them look for the person's field of work, main contributions, nationality, date of work, and any other relevant information. Then have each group conduct a mock interview with the person. To add a writing element, have the groups write a script for the interview. If possible, tape the interviews to help students practice their oral second-language skills. After each group has performed or played back its interview for the class, lead a discussion comparing how the groups highlighted different aspects of the person's personality and career. Post the article and the interview scripts on the bulletin board each week (or as often as you do this activity).

8. Introduce the class to the concept of environmental damage by asking groups to find items in the newspaper that report on or depict sources of pollution. Then have them create a semantic map around the word "pollution," using terms from the newspaper items. When each group has shared its findings with the rest of the class, a large composite map can be created. Ask the class to copy the map; then assign several second-language exercises based on the vocabulary and connections in it. For example, students can write sentences or a short paragraph using as many words as possible from the semantic map or they can write a poem about pollution that incorporates the themes on the map.

9. To teach students how paper is made and to promote the idea of environmental protection, have the class recycle a batch of old newspapers into usable paper. The process is

fairly simple, although it takes several days and some special equipment. Have students follow this five-step procedure:

- Shred several newspapers and stir them into a bucket of water. By the next day, the newspapers will have dissolved into paper pulp.
- Scoop up a portion of the pulp in a grill made of fine wire mesh (with holes no larger than one millimeter) in a wooden frame. This grill will act as a mold and will determine the size of the finished sheet of paper.
- Drain the water from the pulp by gently shaking the grill. This shaking action causes the fibers of the pulp to interlock, creating a mat in the shape of the mold. Make sure there is just enough pulp to make a thin layer (one to two millimeters) in the bottom of the grill. If you have too much or too little, dip the grill back in the water and start again.
- Place the grill with the matted fibers in the sun or close to a source of heat to dry into a sheet of paper.
- When the recycled paper is dry, gently peel it out of the mold and have students write or draw environmental messages on it. The final product can be displayed for the whole school to see.

Social Studies

As in the mathematics and science sections, the activities presented here are not arranged in any specific curriculum sequence. They are divided only by the level of second-language proficiency needed to complete them. Teachers are encouraged to adapt these activities to meet the individual needs of their students in terms of language ability and familiarity with different social studies topics. Teachers should also consider extending these activities whenever possible with techniques such as semantic maps, concept maps, crossword puzzles, and forced combinations. Nearly all of these activities lend themselves to such use, even when this is not specifically noted.

Beginning Activities

1. Have students create an imaginary family using pictures from the newspaper. They can cut out photographs or drawings of people representing all the roles in their imaginary family. With the pictures they can create a collage, labeling each member of the family in English. Then they can write sentences describing the relationships among the family members. A variation of this activity is to create a collage with an extended family arranged in the shape of a genealogical tree. With this type of activity, teachers must be sensitive to the emotional issues that can arise with children who are living with one or neither parent. If desired, different family arrangements can become the topic of a group or class discussion.

2. Ask the class to cut out photographs, drawings, or cartoons that depict community helpers such as firefighters, police officers, mail carriers, paramedics, etc. Then have students work in small groups to choose one picture and create a concept map for that person's function in the community. Each group can then present its concept map to the class. For each map, all the students can construct sentences or short paragraphs describing the relationships shown.

3. For a lesson on the historical development of transportation technology, ask students to cut out newspaper pictures of any means of transportation, (including walking) that are used or have been used by humankind. Students can

then work in groups to paste the pictures on a long sheet of paper, creating a timeline from the earliest forms of transportation to the most recent. Be sure they discuss the placement of each picture before pasting it on the timeline. After each group has reported on its conclusions to the class, the class as a whole can work on a semantic map for the word "transportation."

4. Ask groups of students to search the newspaper for pictures of various transportation mechanisms such as cars, planes, boats, and bicycles. Have them cut out and paste onto a piece of construction paper one example of each type of vehicle. With the students' help, write the name of each vehicle on the chalkboard and have students copy those names and read them aloud. Then ask students to call out the names of different parts of the vehicles in English or in their native language. Write out the English words for the parts and have students copy them to make labels for their pictures. Then ask students to suggest other terms that are associated with the vehicles depicted. With these terms, they can create a semantic or concept map for the word "vehicles."

5. Using any means of communication, including gestures and students' native language, discuss the different kinds of structures that can be found in the newspaper (e.g., apartments, offices, public buildings, houses, stadiums, bridges) and their functions. Ask students to cut out all the types of structures they can find and paste them onto a piece of construction paper. Write the names of the different kinds of structures on the chalkboard and ask students to read them aloud before making labels for their pictures. Then have students name the different parts of those structures, such as door, window, roof, gate, stairs, bleachers, columns, etc. Provide the English words when necessary.

▼ ▼ ▼ ▼ ▼ ▼

If you want, have students use these words to label the different parts of their structures.

6. Introduce the idea of consumer education by having students examine ads for food, cars, clothes, furniture, electronics, and other goods. Have them measure or estimate how much space is devoted to each class of goods. Then have them discuss in small groups why some types of business advertise more than others. What effect do advertisements have on the public? Has anyone in the group ever bought a product because of an ad? Did the product live up to the advertisement? Students can discuss these and related issues in any language; then have each group present a short oral report in English for the rest of the class.

7. The last section presented ways of incorporating environmental issues into lessons focusing on science; however, the environment is also a social issue. Finding a new use for old newspapers presents a perfect opportunity to discuss the impact of recycling and other environmental initiatives on society as a whole and on the way we live. One such use for old newspapers is to convert them into papier-mâché. To do this, first tear pages of the newspaper into one-inch squares. Place the pieces in a pail or other container. Make paste by combining two parts white glue to one part warm water, and add this to the newspaper pieces, stirring until the mixture takes on the consistency of clay. Students can then shape the mixture however they'd like. When the papier-mâché is completely dry, students can decorate it with tempera paint. To give it a shiny finish, students can apply a coat of varnish after the paint has dried.

There are many interesting activities with papier-mâché that can help LEP students develop second-language skills while learning social studies. Since papier-mâché can be manipulated like clay, many kinds of objects can be made with it. For example, students can make jewelry, vases, masks, toys, and other objects that represent a particular culture or time period. They can also make puppets by crumpling a sheet of newspaper into a ball, embedding a finger tube in it, and putting masking tape around it to hold everything together. The tube and ball are then covered with papier-mâché; small pieces of pulp can form ears, nose, mouth, and eyes. Students can attach papier-mâché shoulders to the tube to allow the puppet to hold clothes. When it is dry, students can paint the head, attach hair or a hat, and add appropriate clothes. The puppets can then be used in an English or a bilingual puppet show featuring historic events and people. Puppets can also be used to create a play that addresses multicultural issues; for instance, students can create characters and props for a play that depicts life in different cultures.

Intermediate/Advanced Activities

1. Students can learn about the impact of technology on the modern world by seeking out information about machines and technological inventions in the newspaper. Students can list these inventions in their notebooks and write a short paragraph about each. In the paragraph they should describe what people did (or couldn't do) before that device was invented. Ask students to work cooperatively to put together all the paragraphs and create an image of what life was like before such technological advances were made.

2. Tell students that the class is going to make a time capsule to be opened in 100 years. Working in groups, they will

choose one story from a current newspaper that exemplifies something about today's society. Each group should describe to the class what their article is about and why they chose it for the time capsule. Each member of the group must be responsible for presenting part of the report. To further reinforce language skills, as well as to encourage personal involvement in the project, ask the groups to write a message for the capsule that includes the rationale for their choice of articles and their own view of the aspect of society described. If you want, you can allow students to write part of the message in their native language.

3. To boost students' awareness of propaganda techniques, have them search for ads in the newspaper that make use of techniques such as testimonials (having someone, often a famous person, endorse a product to lend it some prestige), name calling (making a product look good by ridiculing or stressing the weaknesses of a competing product), snob appeal (implying that by using the product the consumer will suddenly become beautiful, powerful, or wealthy), or slanted words or phrases (using marketing or technical jargon to give the product authenticity) to sway consumers. Have groups choose one or two ads and identify the technique used and discuss the intended effect. Each group can display its ad to the class and explain the hidden ideas behind it. If teachers wish, students can write a brief report outlining their conclusions.

4. As a follow-up to the previous activity, have students work in groups to find an ad that uses a different persuasion technique from the ones you presented earlier. Ask them to discuss the intention of the ad's designer. Does the ad appeal to rational arguments or only to feelings? How much does the advertisement have to do with the actual product? How persuasive is the ad? Ask the groups to pre-

sent their conclusions to the rest of the class, with each person reporting on a different aspect. When all the groups are done, ask students to reflect on the information presented and draw some general conclusions. What values are most often espoused in advertising? What assumptions are made (e.g., about the importance of physical appearance)? How do these values and assumptions affect society?

5. After students have become familiar with the format and style of newspaper writing, they can make use of this knowledge to write their own articles. One useful activity is to have them work in groups to choose a historical event and write it up as a short news article. When they're done, they can write a headline and select (or draw) a picture that goes with the story. Each group can display its story on the classroom bulletin board. This activity can be expanded by asking students to write a letter to the editor in the voice of a historical figure or a witness to a historical event.

6. Have students search for pictures of people prominent in politics, entertainment, science, sports, the arts, or some other field and paste the pictures in their notebooks. Then have the class choose one of the best-known personalities and brainstorm words and concepts that are associated with that person (e.g., age, sex, profession, reason for fame, sphere of influence). Use those terms to create a semantic or concept map. Ask the students to write sentences or short paragraphs using the terms in the map. As a follow-up, have students discuss the role and impact of celebrities in society.

7. Display a map of your region, state, or province in the classroom. Ask students to work in groups to find place

names from the area in the news. Each time they find one, have them record it and locate the place on the map. To show that they've found each place on the map, have them write one or two sentences describing the location (e.g., county or other surrounding area, position relative to nearest large city or other landmark). Depending on the students' knowledge of geography, this activity can be expanded to maps of the country or the world.

8. After the students are familiar with the geography of a region, they can trace a map of that area and cut it out. Then they can test their knowledge by filling in the blank map with place names that appear in the newspaper. After they write in the approximate locations of those places, they can work in groups to fill in major features of the map—such as cities, rivers, lakes, and mountains—from memory. Figure 14 shows a map of California completed in this way.

9. Ask students to search the newspaper for news related to protecting the environment and to work in small groups to read and discuss one article. Provide instruction in distinguishing fact from opinion using examples based on the issue of the environment. Then have students write in two separate columns the facts and opinions that can be identified in the article. When they're done, have them analyze the columns and discuss to what extent the opinions expressed are based on the facts presented in the same article. Since this activity is intended to reinforce analytical reading skills more than decoding skills, allow students to use any means of communication to complete the assignment

Figure 14
Activity 8: Geography

Great Central Valley

Sierra Nevada

Lake Tahoe

Sacramento

Oakland

San Francisco

Great Basin

Mojave Desert

Pasadena

Los Angeles

San Diego

REFERENCES

Asher, J.F. (1982). The total physical response approach. In R.W. Blair (Ed.), *Innovative approaches to language learning.* Boston: Newbury House.

Baker, C. (1988). *Key issues in bilingualism and bilingual education.* Clevedon, UK: Multilingual Matters.

Beardsmore, H.B. (1982). *Bilingualism: Basic principles.* Clevedon, UK: Multilingual Matters.

Brown, H.D. (1987). *Principles of language learning and teaching* (2nd ed.). Englewood Cliffs, NJ: Prentice Hall.

Chamot, A.U., & Arambul, B.G. (1985, April). Elementary school science for limited English proficient children. *Focus, 17.* Rosslyn, VA: National Clearinghouse for Bilingual Education.

Cochran, C.E. (1985). *Effective practices for bilingual/esl teachers: Classroom strategies for limited English proficient students.* Trenton, NJ: New Jersey State Department of Education.

Cohen, E.G. (1986). *Designing groupwork: Strategies for the heterogeneous classroom.* New York: Teachers College Press.

Collier, V.P. (1987). The effect of age on acquisition of a second language for school. *New Focus, 1*(2).

Cummins, J. (1981). The role of primary language development in promoting educational success for language minority students. In *Schooling and language minority students: A theoretical framework.* Los Angeles, CA: California State University, Evaluation, Dissemination, and Assessment Center.

De Avila, E.A., Duncan, S.E., & Navarrete, C. (1987). *Finding out/Descubrimiento.* Northvale, NJ: Santillana.

Driver, M. (1979). Cultural diversity and the teaching of science. In H. Trueba & C. Barnett-Mizrachi (Eds.), *Bilingual multicultural education and the professional: From theory to practice.* Boston: Newbury House.

Early, M. (1990). Enabling first and second language learners in the classroom. *Language Arts, 67*(6), 567-575.

Genese, F. (1991). Second language learning in school settings: Lessons from immersion. In A.G. Reynolds (Ed.), *Bilingualism, multiculturalism, and second language learning.* Hillsdale, NJ: Erlbaum.

Hakuta, J., & Snow, C.E. (1986). The role of research in policy decisions about bilingual education. *NABE News 9, 3*(1), 18-21.

Johnson, D.D. (1981). *An investigation of the relationship between prior knowledge, vocabulary development, and passage comprehension with culturally diverse children.* Madison, WI: University of Wisconsin, Center for Educational Research.

Kagan, S. (1986). *Beyond language: Social and cultural factors in schooling language minority students.* Los Angeles, CA: California State University, Evaluation, Dissemination, and Assessment Center.

Kagan, S. (1987). *Cooperative learning resources for teachers.* Riverside, CA: University of California.

Krashen, S. (1981). *Second language acquisition and second language learning.* Oxford, UK: Pergamon.

Krashen, S. (1982). *Principles and practice in second language acquisition.* Oxford, UK: Pergamon.

Langrehr, J. (1988). *Teaching students to think.* Bloomington, IN: National Education Service.

Langrehr, J. (1990). *Sharing thinking strategies.* Bloomington, IN: National Educational Service.

Larsen-Freeman, D. (1991). Second language acquisition research: Staking out the territory. *TESOL Quarterly, 25*(2), 315-350.

Lessow-Hurley, J. (1990). *The foundations of dual language instruction.* White Plains, NY: Longman.

Levine, L.N. (1985). Content area instruction for the elementary school ESL student. In P. Larson, E.L. Judd, & D.S. Messerschmitt (Eds.), *On TESOL '84: A brave new world for TESOL.* Washington, DC: TESOL, Georgetown University.

McGroarty, M. (1989). The benefits of cooperative learning arrangements in second language instruction. *NABE Journal, 13*(2), 127-143.

Mohan, B.A. (1986). *Language and content.* Reading, MA: Addison-Wesley.

Ovando, C.J., & Collier, V.P. (1985). *Bilingual and ESL classrooms: Teaching in a multicultural context.* New York: McGraw-Hill.

Rodriguez, R. (1986). Reading comprehension instructional strategies: Aids for the bilingual reader. In R. Rodriguez (Series Ed.), *Teaching reading to minority language students.* Rosslyn, VA: Interamerican Research Associates.

Romero, M. (1991). Transitional bilingual education: An instructional perspective. In A. Carrasquillo (Ed.), *Bilingual education: Using languages for success.* New York: New York State Association for Bilingual Education.

Ruiz, R. (1991). The empowerment of language-minority students. In C.E. Sleeter (Ed.), *Empowerment through multicultural education.* Albany, NY: State University of New York Press.

Savignon, S. (1991). Communicative language teaching: State of the art. *TESOL Quarterly, 25*(2), 261-277.

Secada, W.G. (1989). Innovative strategies for teaching mathematics to limited English proficient students. *Program information guide series, number 10.* Rosslyn, VA: National Clearinghouse for Bilingual Education.

Short, D. (1988). *Preparing to integrate language and content instruction: A training manual.* Washington, DC: Center for Applied Linguistics.

Slavin, R.E. (1983). *Cooperative learning.* White Plains, NY: Longman.

Sutman, F.X., Allen, V.F., & Shoemaker, F. (1986). *Learning English through science.* Washington, DC: National Science Teachers Association.

Swain, M. (1985). Communicative competence: Some roles of comprehensible input and comprehensible output in its development. In S. Gass & C. Madden (Eds.), *Input in second language acquisition.* Boston: Newbury House.

Thonis, E.W. (1981). Reading instruction for language minority students. In *Schooling and language minority students: A theoretical framework.* Los Angeles, CA: California State University, Evaluation, Dissemination, and Assessment Center.

Other Resources for Using Newspapers in Education

A number of teachers' guides are available for ESL and mainstream teachers interested in using newspapers to educate LEP students. However, that material needs to be adapted for use in the classroom since most ESL activities suggested in the literature were developed for adults. Teachers of kindergarten to grade 12 will find that few of these teaching guides address the needs of elementary and secondary students.

There has been no body of work that discusses the use of the newspaper to integrate language and content area learning. Since this book is the first such work, the activities presented in the resources that follow must be adapted to the characteristics of a classroom that includes language minority students. For help in making this adaptation effectively, see the methodological recommendations in chapters 2 and 4.

General Education

Bibliography of Newspapers in Education. (1991). This is the most complete list of resources available for the use of newspapers in education. It lists 300 publications on this topic, both by theme and alphabetically. Each entry includes the author, a description of the content, applicable grade levels, number of activities, price, number of pages, and ordering information. Published by the Newspaper Association of America (NAA) Foundation. Available from: Newspaper in Education, NAA Foundation, 11600 Sunrise Valley Drive, Reston, VA 22091.

Teacher's Curriculum Guide for Newspaper in Education Week. (annual publication). A curriculum guide offering a new topic each year to enhance newspaper instruction in the classroom. Available from: International Reading Association, 800 Barksdale Rd., PO Box 8139, Newark, DE 19714-8139.

English as a Second Language

English by Newspaper. (1984). T.L. Fredrickson & P.F. Wedel. A 180-page book full of activities to improve English reading abilities using the newspaper. The book was developed for self-study to reinforce the ability to read and understand an English-language newspaper. Most of the exercises can be adapted to classroom activities with advanced ESL students. Available in bookstores or directly from the publisher: Newbury House, 20 Park Plaza, Boston, MA 02116.

English as a Second Language. (1988). F. Belge & N. Slowi. (J. Britton, Ed.). Includes 60 pages of activities for learning ESL through the newspaper, from beginning to advanced levels. Appropriate for use with students in K to 12. Available from: *The Syracuse Newspaper,* Director of Educational Services, PO Box 4915, Syracuse, NY 13221.

Note: All addresses are in the United States unless otherwise indicated.

English as a Second Language Newspaper Activities. (1986). J. Byer & J. Gunther. A selection of activities for grades 4 to 12 focusing on second-language skills and mainstream culture. Available from: *Kansas City Star/Times,* Newspaper in Education Manager, 11729 Grand Ave., Kansas City, MO 64108.

ESL—*English as a Second Language.* (1985). Classroom activities to develop second language skills for grades K to 6. Available only with a four-week newspaper order from: *The Star Ledger,* Newspaper in Education Coordinator, Star Ledger Plaza, Newark, NJ 07101.

The Houston Chronicle—Your ESL Source. (1989). A teacher's guide for adult education in ESL. Describes activities with the newspaper to develop listening, speaking, reading, and writing skills. Most activities can be adapted for upper elementary, middle school, and high school grades. Available from: *The Houston Chronicle,* Education Services Department, 801 Texas Ave., Houston, TX 77002.

Language for Living. (1985). A seven-page manual for teaching survival skills in handling things like money, legal issues, and transportation. The manual was developed for adults, but it can be adapted for use with high school students. Available from: Promotional and Educational Services, Canadian Newspaper Publishers Association, 3212 Bloor St. E., Suite 214, Toronto, Ont., Canada M4W 1E7.

The Newspaper for Second Language Learners. (1986). B. Sullivan, B. Duncan, & H. Moore-Servillo, Eds. Twenty-five teaching ideas for using the newspaper with beginning to advanced LEP students in all grades. Available from: *Newsday,* Senior Education Coordinator, 2 Park Ave., New York, NY 10016.

The Newspaper and You. (1980). D. Golder. Basic reading skills adapted specifically for ESL students. Can be used with elementary, middle school, or high school students with varying levels of second-language proficiency. Available from: AMSCO School Publications, 315 Hudson St., New York, NY 10013.

Not Born in the USA! (1987). K. O'Malley. Learning activities focusing on ESL and cultural awareness for secondary or adult students born outside the U.S. Available from: *The Central New Jersey Home News,* NIE Consultant, 123 How Ln., New Brunswick, NJ 07013.

Teaching English as a Second Language with the Los Angeles Times. (1989). B. Allor, A. Coleman, M. Fernandez, C. Marquez, & W. Miller (M.H. House, Ed. and Prod.). Activities for teaching ESL using all sections of the newspaper. These activities can be adapted for different levels of English language proficiency. Available by telephoning *Los Angeles Times* in Education, 1-800-528-4637, ext. 74342 (in Orange County, ext. 67740).

Upper ESL and Amnesty Preparation: The Daily News in Adult Education. (1988). Lesson plans and worksheets for all levels of ESL instruction, as well as U.S. citizenship education and employment preparation. These lessons were developed for use with adults, but they can be adapted for middle school and high school students. Available from: *Los Angeles Daily News,* PO Box 4200, Woodland Hills, CA 91365.

Mathematics

Classroom Va-Voom. (1985). M. Dumpy. Mathematics activities using the newspaper that cover a broad spectrum of higher-level competencies. The activities are designed specifically to help students achieve the Florida Standards of Excellence in Math for grades 3 to 5. Several activities can be adapted for use with LEP students. Available from: FNIEC Inc., PO Drawer 1949, Jacksonville, FL 32231.

Mathematics + Newspaper = Learning + Fun. (1982). E.J. Sowell & R.J. Casey. In *Mathematics for the Middle Grades (5-9),* L. Sivey, Ed. This article suggests five mathematics lessons that make use of the newspaper. They can be adapted for use with

LEP students in grades 5 to 9. Available in libraries or from the publisher: National Council of Teachers of Mathematics, 1906 Association Dr., Reston, VA 22091-1593.

Math Skills Activities. (1983). Fifty activities to reinforce, practice, and maintain basic math skills by using the newspaper. These activities were developed for native English speakers, but they can be adapted to reinforce second-language skills while introducing mathematics concepts. Available from: *The Peoria Journal Star,* Director/Educational Services, One New Plaza, Peoria, IL 61643.

Newspapers and Mathematics. (1989). Classroom math activities for different grades. Developed for native English speakers, but can be adapted to help LEP students develop math and second-language skills. Available from: The Newspaper Society, Bloomsbury House, 74-77 Great Russell St., London WC1B 3DA, England.

That Figures. (1986). M. Hintz & J. Ziegler. Forty mathematics activities with the newspaper. Themes include fractions, percentages, graphs, scientific notation, and basic arithmetic operations. Developed for mainstream students, but can be adapted for LEP students in grades 6 to 10. Available from: *The Kitchener-Waterloo Record,* 225 Fairway Rd., Kitchener, Ont., Canada N2G 4E5.

Science

Science and Newspapers. (1985). M. Mansour. This publication includes several activities that can be adapted for use with LEP students. The language component can be stressed when working on activities that distinguish observations from inferences or when discussing physical properties, new technologies, and other topics addressed here. These activities are appropriate for students in the elementary grades. Available from: *Detroit Free Press,* Educational Services Management, 321 W. Lafayette Blvd., Detroit, MI 48231.

Social Studies

Newschool: Using the Newspaper to Teach Social Studies.
(1985). M. Olson. Many of the activities in this teacher's guide,
developed for the mainstream classroom, can be adapted for use
with LEP students in grades 4 and up. Available from: Dale
Seymor Publications, PO Box 10888, Palo Alto, CA 94303.

Social Studies. (1986). D. Roberts. This teacher's guide suggests activities for using the newspaper to develop several basic
skills in social studies. Developed for mainstream students, these
activities can be adapted for nonnative English speakers in grades
K to 8. Available from: Newspaper in Education, *The Arizona
Republic/The Phoenix Gazette,* PO Box 1950, Phoenix, AZ
85001.

▼ ▼ ▼ ▼ ▼ ▼

Also available from IRA...

Teaching Reading Skills through the Newspaper (third edition) by Arnold B. Cheyney is a handy guide to using the newspaper to help students at all levels learn about reading while studying the realities of day-to-day living. With this book and a newspaper, teachers will have plenty of ideas and activities that will challenge and excite students for hours. The newspaper — an inexpensive, widely available, topical, and flexible resource — is one of the most relevant texts available for the classroom, and its "user-friendly" format makes the information it contains easily accessible to readers. Over 50,000 copies of previous editions of this book have been sold. Here, Cheyney provides dozens of new teaching tips that will help students with reading while they learn about the world around them.

To order your copy of *Teaching Reading Skills through the Newspaper,* call 1-800-336-READ, ext. 266 (outside North America, call 302-731-1600, ext. 266). Visa and MasterCard accepted; shipping included on prepaid orders.

Teaching Reading Skills through the Newspaper
1992   64 pages   softcover
IRA book no. 236-622   ISBN 0-87207-236-3
IRA members US$4.00; nonmembers US$6.00